SIXTY YEARS A PREACHER.

RICHARD LEE.

MY DIAMOND JUBILEE:
SIXTY YEARS
A PREACHER
OF THE GOSPEL.

RICHARD LEE.

J. STARR & SONS, LTD., WIGAN.

—

1923.

PREFACE.

There are many voices calling to us to-day. As the years come and go, these voices increase in number and volume. The Church calls us to fields of service; reformers plead for our aid; earth's woes call to us for redress; but above them all, yet mingling with them all, sounds one loud clear voice—the voice of the Master.

I have heard that voice, and in obedience to its call have given 60 years of my life to the Ministry of the Gospel in the Churches with which I have throughout my life been associated. God has been graciously pleased to own my service, and to crown it with success, in that He has used me to bring help and blessing to many.

I shall shortly enter my eightieth year, and am deeply grateful that God in His goodness has granted me such health that even yet I am able, week by week, to travel to my appointments in Churches widely separated in point of distance, therein to preach the Gospel and unfold the riches of His grace.

I make no pretence to literary gifts. The only elementary education I ever received in a public day school was during six weeks I spent in one of them. Reading and writing, as well as the Scriptures, were taught in the Sunday School, and there my interest was awakened. As I was

ILLUSTRATIONS.

—

SIXTY YEARS A PREACHER.

A SHEAF OF FRIENDLY MESSAGES.

When intimation was made by our friend Richard Lee, through the Connexional Magazine and elsewhere, of his intention to publish a memorial volume of his sixty years' service as a Minister of the Gospel of Christ, there were many who desired to send to him messages of gratitude and goodwill. The letters received have been handed over to a friend to do with what he will. Space is not available for more than selected passages, except in one or two instances. Such an instance is that of the Connexional Committee, the communication which follows speaking for many past and present members of that Committee who would otherwise have written personal letters.

MESSAGES FROM REPRESENTATIVE BODIES.

A MESSAGE OF GREETING AND REMEMBRANCE FROM THE CONNEXIONAL COMMITTEE.

Dear Brother Lee,

Your friends and colleagues of the Connexional Committee have learned with much interest that you have nearly completed sixty years' service as a Minister of the Gospel. They are happy to remember that during this long period of service your strength has been unstintingly given to the Churches of our own denomination, and that apart from your special service as a preacher, you have carried much personal sympathy and a ministry of comfort to many.

They remember also with much satisfaction that your time and thought have been given very freely to our smaller Churches, which have been greatly cheered and heartened by your constant visits and affectionate interest.

It is with pleasure that they record their appreciation of the many sacrifices made in order that such a ministry might be sustained, their sense of the value of your friendly counsel and constant efforts for the peace and harmony of our Church and Connexional life.

They record, too, with deep gratitude and reverence, their appreciation of a life marked by singleness of purpose and devotion to the highest ends, and give thanks to God that they have been able so long to share your welcome fellowship and many kindnesses.

It is the prayer of your many friends and fellow-labourers that you may have the joy of giving many more years of fruitful service, and carrying to the Churches the fruits of your ripe experience and character.

Signed on behalf of the Connexional Committee,

THOMAS LOMAX, President.
HENRY BARRETT, Secretary.

From the Wigan and District Independent Methodist Churches.

This tribute to our brother Richard Lee's sixty years' faithful, devoted and loyal service is specifically a Circuit or District one. We are not, however, unmindful of the distinguished services he has rendered to our own religious fellowship especially, such as being its President for two years, successively, an Evangelist for a number of years, a member of the Executive for nearly a generation, and the representative of the Denomination at the Ecumenical Conference, at Toronto, in October, 1911.

Nor would we forget the great service he has rendered to other religious bodies and kindred institutions, such as the Free Church Council, the Y.M.C.A. Movement, the Women's Auxiliary, various Temperance Organisations, etc. It is, however, from a Circuit point of view that we would express the deepest personal regard we all feel towards him, and our high appreciation of a long life unfalteringly given to the service of Christ. For sixty years our friend has been identified with one and the same Circuit ; for the first few years of his ministry with what was then the Bolton and Wigan Circuit. About the year 1871, by mutual agreement, two Circuits were formed out of this area, and truly the division of interest and responsibility has been a blessing to both. Since then Brother Lee has held unbroken association with the Wigan Circuit, so that he has to his credit a continuity of service in one Circuit for sixty years, a thing of which any man might justly be proud.

For these three score years Bro. Lee has been engaged

in the most important of all work in the Master's service, the preaching of the everlasting Word of Life to fallen humanity. His zeal does not flag owing to his years; if anything, he exhibits a greater keenness as he grows older, especially in regard to the young folk, for, as he himself says, having experienced what God has done for him both in youth and middle age, and, as we must add, in old age, he can with confidence say that the same true and living God will in some measure do the same for all young people.

Brother Lee has been Treasurer since the death of James Proe more than twenty years ago. In this capacity he has, indeed, done most valuable service. He has also been one of the Circuit Representatives on the Connexional Committee for a quarter of a century, and still represents us thereon.

A word must be said about his dear wife. Only he knows how much he is indebted to her for the sacrifices she must have made, for her words of encouragement and helpfulness, which have enabled him to do the work which he has so lovingly undertaken. It is our prayer that both may be spared yet many years, and that each may in the Father's own time be granted a happy entrance to the City of our God.

On behalf of the Wigan and District Independent
Methodist Churches,

Signed,

W. HURST, President.
T. PERRY, Secretary.

WIGAN AND DISTRICT FREE CHURCH COUNCIL.

Copy of Resolution unanimously passed at its Meeting, on Friday, May 4th, 1923.

MR. RICHARD LEE'S DIAMOND JUBILEE.

" That this Council desires to express its sincere congratulations to Mr. Richard Lee on his attaining his Diamond Jubilee as a preacher of the Gospel. It recalls with joy the fact that Mr. Lee has been connected with the Council from its formation, having taken part in the inaugural meetings leading to the founding of the National Council. For some years Mr. Lee was Treasurer of the Council, and also served two terms as President. He rendered invaluable service by conducting a series of Evangelistic meetings during the Simultaneous Mission in 1901. Mr. Lee has represented the local Council on several occasions at the Annual Gatherings of the National Council, and he has also been honoured by his appointment as President of the South-West Lancashire Federation of Free Church Councils. He has always taken a deep interest in all the work of the Council, and in the furtherance of all good causes, and the Council prays that he may still have many years of gracious service for the Master he loves and represents so faithfully."

Signed,

EMMANUEL TAYLOR, J.P., President.
S. G. JENKINS, Secretary.

benefited by the sacrificial devotion of your labours in the
cause of the Kingdom.   Through all the years of our happy
association with you, we younger men have learned to
honour and to love you.   We have seen in you the infre-
quent miracle happen—we have watched you grow younger
as years advanced, and heard in you the voice of God
speaking to us with the wisdom of a rich experience and the
heart of a little child.   Your book cannot tell us much
that we do not know, but because we feel that those who
have not been blessed as we have, with the personal and
direct touch, may gather something of the inspiration
which your life has brought to us, we welcome it.   The
tale of the years you have spent is already told, and there
will be more yet to tell."

HARTLEY BARRETT, Nelson.

" I should just like, if you will allow me, to say how helpful your life has been to me.   As far back as I can remember
your commanding presence, with its gracious influence,
has been a potent factor in my life, but it was when I came
into more intimate relationship with you that I realised
more and more the sterling strength of your character.   I
should like to thank you most sincerely for the kind recep-
tion you gave me, when, as a youth, I came on to the
Connexional Committee, on taking up the responsible
position of Finance Secretary to the Connexion.   Your
appreciation and kindly expressions have helped me very
considerably all along ;   your very presence always gives
me strength and inspiration."

RUSHTON SILSON, Birkdale.

" It was in the year 1899 when, as a scholar in Greenough Street Sunday School, I first came under the influence of your ministry at a Sunday evening service. In your own home I was led by you through prayer to the foot of the Cross, there to take my stand for Christ, and afterwards work for the Church, of which I became a minister, and in that capacity served the Church faithfully for twenty years. Let me say that right through the whole of my Christian life your influence has kept me faithful, and guided me through many difficulties."

F. MAKIN, Bolton.

" I remember you speaking at the Annual Conference, held at our Church, at Noble Street, Bolton, 45 years ago. I especially remember one sermon you preached on ' Faith,' some 30 years ago. To illustrate one of your points you offered a silver coin to any in the congregation who would accept it. One of my scholars came for the coin, and the incident lives with him yet."

A. WINNARD, Beecher House, Wigan.

" As an Independent Methodist, I can pay tribute to the devoted service rendered by Mr. Lee as a minister.

To live under the shadow of a good man and woman is indeed a privilege. It has fallen to my lot to enjoy such a privilege under varying conditions of life. For that I am thankful, and place upon record my appreciation and

have received of your sixty years' service. It is with little
less than a feeling of awe that we permit our thoughts to
rest upon the old school in ' The Square,' as it was about
seventy years ago. There in imagination we see you as a
boy of ten years drinking in eagerly words of grace which
fell from the lips of men and women of simple life and
thought. Ten years pass, and we see you as a stripling
preaching the first of many thousand sermons from the old
pulpit, amongst those listening to you being some in all
probability who were present at the beginnings of our
Church more than a century ago. Our thoughts travel
onward, and we see a great procession of boys and girls,
men and women, who during the visits of sixty years have
heard your appeals, which, in some measure, have always
been answered as soon as spoken, in the emotions of the
heart. And still God speaks to us through you ; speaks
to us, perhaps, most of all through your personality. In
our hearts there is a blending of love, of reverence, and of
gratitude, and we pray that to you and your beloved wife
there may be given a deeper sense of God's love and grace
until the call comes and you go to meet your Pilot face to
face."—G. CHALLENDER.

INTRODUCTION.

By Edward Ralphs.

Though the interest of this book will appeal mainly to the large circle of friends who have enjoyed a living intimacy with Richard Lee, it is possible that it may fall into the hands of many who may not have intimate knowledge of the denomination which he has so faithfully served as a minister for such an unusually long period as sixty years.

The Connexion of Independent Methodists came into being not quite 120 years ago, comprising then, and for many years afterwards, a very few Churches. Richard Lee's active ministerial life, therefore, covers about half the history of the denomination. A phrase often used to define the nature of its witness is " A Free Church and a Free Ministry." The spiritual principle underlying this is " the priesthood of all believers." It has never been found possible in these churches to reconcile this principle with the exclusive, or to all intents and purposes exclusive, pastorate of the single church. It is held to imply the absolute equality of all the members of a church, in right, in privilege, and in obligation ; that no office or function in the church may be exercised by one that may not be exercised by all if suitably gifted ; that all barriers should be removed which prevent the full and free exercise of the varied gifts of the members of the church ; that the pulpit, along with every other avenue of service, should be open to whoever the church deems fit ; that as, in every church there may be several endowed by God with preaching power the pulpit cannot be reserved for any one person, as pastor without interfering with the freedom of the Spirit's call. One principle is therefore held as vital— the preservation of an open pulpit. The natural corollary of a diverse and multiplied ministry in the individual church is that it should be voluntary and unpaid, and this has come to be recognised as the chief feature in its polity, and is jealously guarded and strenuously upheld. They gladly recognise and welcome the fact that God has so gifted certain men and women, that it is desirable they should devote their whole time to the specific work of evangelism and the building up of weak churches, and that during such service it is right that they should be maintained. This service, or ministry, however, is to be so exercised that it shall not hinder the full exercise by others of their gifts, but shall encourage and stimulate their development. The evangelistic ministry of the denomination stands this test, as it is in no sense exclusive.

It may be that because I have had a life-long association with the church Richard Lee joined sixty-four years ago that my friend has asked me to contribute this introduction. I do so with much pleasure and a feeling of gratitude that it has been my joy to know and to love him from my childhood. One of the weekly events of my early boyhood days was the visit to his shop for the magazines my father and mother got regularly, and which I read with as much avidity as they did. His ministry began when I was a child in my mother's arms.

The church of his early years has a notable history of its own. Its founders were men of evangelical and reforming zeal. Some of them walked 26 miles to Manchester and back to attend the Peterloo Meeting, in 1819, and this brought about a crisis in the religious Society of which they were members, the Superintendent Minister raising strong objection to their political views and tendencies. One of these men was George Hodson, who became one of the first ministers of Wingates Church. He was born in 1788, and lived until about 1874. I heard him preach occasionally as a boy of from seven to ten years. Hodson told the minister that they could preach and pray for themselves, and another man named Bamber said there could be no such thing as spiritual freedom where there was political thraldom. The church came into being, and was represented at the Annual Conference just a hundred years ago, in 1823, by my own grandfather, Edward Basnett, who was one of its first preachers. To this church came Peter Phillips and many others of the Warrington and Manchester preachers more than a hundred years ago. There were no trains, trams or buses, or even horses at their disposal. They quite frequently walked 30 miles, conducted two and sometimes three services on the Sunday, and were absent from home 18 or 20 hours, but back at the loom or other work next morning. With very few exceptions they were workmen who earned too little for even moderate comfort, and it is impossible to withhold admiration for these men of sturdy, independent spirit, and the splendid pioneer work they did. They had few books, but they were students of life and of the Scriptures, and they carried a living message. They did not despise education; they desired it, and when there were no day schools in the villages they taught writing and reading in the Sunday Schools, and built up small school libraries.

It was such a Sunday School as this that Richard Lee attended as a boy at Wingates, the girl who became his wife also attending as a scholar at the same time. Through his wife his family associations go back practically to the beginnings of the church, for Thomas Boardman, his wife's father, was baptised there on July 22nd, 1822. Richard was deeply interested in religious matters, even in his early teens. He kept a note-book, and jotted down the texts and some of the things the preachers said, for the desire was already born in him to become a preacher too. He was not even out of his teens before he had begun to preach, and it is notable that it was a woman preacher who stirred up the gift within him. He tells the story on another page. The Mrs. Butler he refers to was a Wingates woman of considerable natural gifts, whom I frequently heard preach. There was never any prejudice against women preachers in a church of so democratic an origin. They were fully enfranchised from the beginning. It may be said in passing that when Mrs. Butler died, in 1895, Richard Lee very fittingly took part in the service of interment and preached the memorial sermon. An old friend wrote to me when she died: "Nanny Butler has entered into my life, and I can see a very serious soul looking out of a fair casket, and applying my ear to memory's phonograph, I can distinctly hear her voice in earnest prayer pleading for souls to be saved."

These things are worth recalling, because they show the sort of people among whom Richard Lee spent his early years, and the stimulating quality of the spiritual atmosphere he breathed. It has seemed to him a perfectly natural thing that for sixty years he should put his whole soul into the work of preaching the Gospel freely. Sixty years a preacher! Something like 6,000 sermons and addresses delivered! What deep significance such simple phrases as these carry with them! Evenings and week-ends for 60 years joyously spent in the best of all services—the winning of men and women, of boys and girls, for the Christian life, and the service of Christ. Think of the churches visited, the friendships formed, the memories treasured, the gratitude felt by the hundreds who by him were led into the light, the influence of a life always lived upon a high plane, the joy of sharing both his material and spiritual possessions with others, and always moved by a deep conviction that the Christ he served had the needful word for all our ills, personal and social. What but grati-tude, and reverence too, can any of us feel?

A considerable part of this book consists of sermonettes or sermon outlines. I have read every word of them with pleasure and profit. They are characteristic of the man—simple in form, but full of a loving concern, and of an intense desire to make us realise the vital import of the Christian message and the essential simplicity of the Gospel. Our friend leaves purely theological matters alone, and is wise in doing so. He eschews biblical criticism, and again is wise. For none of it affects the spiritual and ethical value of the scriptures. But this is not to say that he does not touch the deep things. He touches nothing but the deep things: The Love of God—The true way of Life—The fact of Sin—Of the release from Sin's power—

C

ceased to be an Evangelist, he commenced in January, 1885, a restaurant in Wigan, and speedily laid the foundation of a successful business. He clung to Dicconson Lane Church until 1892, when he and his wife transferred their membership to Greenough-St. Church, Wigan. For 1893-4-5 he served as Connexional Treasurer. Then he was elected Vice-President in 1896, and for 1897–8 filled the office of President. Since then he has continued a member of the Connexional Committee, representing Wigan Circuit, in late years being the Chairman of the Visiting Committee. In 1898, when Wigan Circuit decided to establish Kendal Street Church, he settled there and has made it his chief concern. When the new chapel was built he and his wife gave a donation of £500 to the building fund. In March, 1916, they again remembered the church at their golden wedding, when offerings to the amount of £60 were made to the church by their many friends to commemorate the event, 300 guests being present to partake of their hospitality. At the Methodist Ecumenical Conference, held in America, in October, 1911, Mr. Lee was one of our representatives, and gave an address. Some years ago he visited the Holy Land, and has given many interesting addresses on his experiences during the tour. He and his wife are still amongst us, and held in honour.

———

After I became President of the Connexion, in 1897, the editor of *The Wingates Messenger* sought an interview with me because of my Wingates associations, and in the August issue of that year he published the following, which in somewhat fuller detail amplifies some of the incidents referred to by Mr. Vickers.

From The Wingates Messenger, August, 1897.

We have considerable pleasure in presenting our readers with a photograph of Mr. Richard Lee, of Wigan, who, by an unanimous vote, has been chosen President of our Connexion. On no more worthy shoulders has the mantle of the Presidency yet fallen. He is an old Wingates boy, and Wingates feels that any honour conferred upon any of her children is also conferred upon her.

Perhaps the following brief notes of a conversation the editor had with Bro. Lee a few days ago may find acceptance with our readers. We regret that the space at our disposal forbids more :—

" I suppose Wingates Church, Bro. Lee, may really claim you as one of her old boys ? "

" Yes, that is the case. I received my earliest and best impressions at Wingates. I am sure I will never forget Joseph Gregory. He was the first to show any interest in my spiritual welfare. I lived then at the Old Tollbar, at the top of Dicconson Lane, and when I was a lad, about ten years of age, he came up one day and invited myself and five others to the Sunday School. We promised we would go, and kept our word."

" Joseph Gregory did more that day than he thought, in giving that simple invitation to half-a-dozen careless lads."

" I presume educational advantages were few in your boyish days ? "

" They were, indeed. When I was eight years of age I went to work down the coal mine. I worked as a collier

" You are now a member of Greenough Street Church, Wigan ? "

" Yes ; my wife and I continued our membership at Dicconson Lane until five years ago, when we felt we could transfer our membership without the church at Dicconson Lane suffering much. But even now I am in a church with which Wingates is honourably associated. John Fell and George Hodson, two of the earliest preachers at Wingates, had no mean share in establishing what is now one of the most successful churches in the connexion, viz : Greenough Street."

" And the future of our connexion, Bro. Lee,—what is your view ? "

" A very hopeful one. I think the future of our body is very promising."

And here our notes of the interview must end.

MY CONVERSION.

In the preceding interview, my conversion is referred to as taking place when I was a youth of 14 years. It may be useful if I tell the story a little more fully.

I go back to a certain Sunday night service, in the Old Chapel at Wingates, Westhoughton. John Birchall, of Lowton, was the preacher, and all through the service God seemed to be speaking to me. A Prayer Meeting was announced to be held at the close of the service, and a Cottage Prayer Meeting the Wednesday following. When the Prayer Meeting was commenced, sitting near my companion, I said : " John, shall we stay ? " He said : " Yes." Having felt the drawing influence all through the service, it became overpowering in the prayer meeting, and for the first time in public I prayed.

I had been in the school and attending the preaching service for some years, and I was not ignorant of the plan of salvation. I knew there must be a willingness on my part to receive what Christ was so anxious to give, and that night I decided to give myself to God and His service.

That is 65 years ago. I have never regretted the step I took that night, and I thank God for converting and keeping grace.

I must now go back to the Sunday Night Prayer Meeting, and the first time I had prayed in public.

My companion, John Young, lived in the same village, about a mile from the Chapel. We walked home, and neither of us uttered a word until we got to the village, and it came to saying good-night. But before I could say good-night, I felt I must say something else. So I said: "John, I don't know what you think of what I have done to-night. I felt that I could not leave the meeting until I had made it known that I had decided for God. I should have decided sooner but I have been afraid of you."

Then John said: "That is strange, very strange, for I have been afraid of you." Then I said: "Shall we go to the Cottage Prayer Meeting on Wednesday, at White Horse?" and he said: "Yes;" and that night he prayed and decided for God.

Here are companions loving each other, both under the influence of God's Spirit, yet afraid to talk about the life they were both anxious to live.

writings have been of great value to me. After all, Paul's advice to young Timothy, to give attention to reading, is the best possible advice for preachers, not only at the beginning of one's ministry, but continually to the end. It was partly because I loved good books, and wished others to love them too, that when I left the coal mine I went from house to house selling Bibles, Bunyan's Works, The Life of Christ, and other literature of like character, in good editions, and I found a great readiness, in the humblest homes, to buy books of good standard quality. This naturally led to my opening out as a bookseller, stationer and photographer, etc.

As to methods of preparation, it was my habit to mark passages that struck my attention as I read. I came back to these afterwards, and they served as seed thoughts which I meditated upon and expanded in my own way, and it is from notes such as these that the sermonettes given elsewhere in this book have been mainly compiled. As to the matter of delivery of sermons, this is, of course, of very great importance. Naturally possessing a strong voice, I was not content with this only, but went to a Congregational Minister, who lived in Westhoughton when I began preaching, and to him I read passages from books, and he criticised my expression. I do know this : that having really tried, through reading, meditation and prayer, to prepare helpful messages for the people to whom I have ministered, God has blessed the spoken word, and I shall be happy if the printed word may also be a means of blessing to any who may read.

JIM AND I.

It has been suggested to me by a friend to whom I related the story recently that I should include in this narrative the story of " Jim and I."

Jim was a Westhoughton boy attending our Sunday School at Wingates. He was a scholar in the same class and about my age. He left Westhoughton, and went to live with an uncle at Ashton-in-Makerfield. Ashton, at this time, was a noted place for lock making. I suppose Jim became a lock-maker. For many years I did not see him. He married a Westhoughton girl. He got away from the Sunday School in his early teens, and after his marriage, if not before, he began, like many others, to go to the public house and have his one glass. But the time came when he became a drunkard.

His wife died, and after that he went from bad to worse. I did not see much of him until he was about 55 years of age, when I met him in Wigan going into a public house. He was then the worse for drink. I put my hand on his shoulder, and I said : " Jim, I am sorry to see you in this state. I wish I could help you, for your uncle's sake." Then Jim began to cry. I have referred to the Westhoughton uncle with whom he lived when a boy, and until he went to Ashton. This uncle was the man who induced me and five other boys to attend the Sunday School, at Wingates, Westhoughton. Jim knew that his uncle was a good man, and when I mentioned his name that caused him to weep. Yet he went forward into the public house.

Two or three weeks after this I saw him again in Wigan. This time he crossed the street to speak to me, but for a

time he was speechless. So I said : " What is it, Jim ? "
Then he said : " Could you give me an old pair of boots ? "
I said : " I am going by train, which is almost due ; will you
come to our house in the morning, and be there about
nine o'clock ? "   Jim was at our door at the hour named,
and when he went away he had not only boots but a fairly
good suit. My clothes fitted him all right. Boots, cap, and
all complete, and he looked respectable. You will understand his condition when I say that the clothes he came in
were thrown over the wall for the rag gatherer to pick up.

Jim was going away thanking us when I called him back
and put a piece of silver in his hand, saying : " You know I am
a teetotaler, Jim."   " Aye, I know you are, and I wish I had
been one."   Then I said : " If you spend any of that in
drink, and I get to know, I shall be very much hurt."   " I
will never touch it again while I live," he said.   I am sorry
to say Jim did not keep his promise.

I did not see him again for 8 or 9 weeks, and I was beginning to think he was keeping sober and working. I was
consoling myself, thinking I had helped him to a better life,
for I was anxious to save him. Again I saw him in Wigan
in a worse condition, if that is possible, than he was when
I clothed him from head to foot. He must have pawned
the clothes. He tried to avoid me, but I went to him and
had another talk with him.

The Free Church Council of Wigan and District have had
a short service in our Wigan Workhouse on Sunday after-
noons for more than 20 years. I have taken part in that
service many times, and being near our Kendal Street
Church a part of our choir have accompanied me, and we

have had good times.   The second or third time of preaching
in the Workhouse, as I stood in the pulpit while singing the
opening hymn, I noticed a man hiding his face with his cap.
It is a long room, with the pulpit about the centre, the men
to the left, and the women just a little to the right.   When
we had sung and prayed, and read a short portion of the
scripture, and sung another hymn out of Sankey's book,
and I had been talking perhaps a few minutes, the cap
dropped, and the man was weeping.   I knew it was Jim
from the first, but seeing he was no longer disposed to hide
himself, I said : " There is a man over there I know ; you
will excuse me, won't you, Jim ? " He said, : " Go on,
sir."   So I went on, and made mention of his uncle who had
been so helpful to me and the man who induced me to attend
when a boy the Sunday School.   This was a short time after
seeing him in the street, when he tried to avoid me, and
about three months after having clothed him.

My next visit to the Workhouse, to take part in the
service, was only a few weeks after.   I did not see Jim, but
I made enquiry, and was told that he was still there, but
not well.   I have every reason to believe that he died in
the Workhouse.   That is 20 years ago.   I cannot follow
him any further, but I would leave him with the One who
pardoneth iniquity because He delighteth in mercy.

Without saying anything of the life after death, I like
to think of the advantages in this life between those who
serve God and those who do not serve Him.

If there is any difference between Jim and myself, what
makes the difference ?

Rev. 3 : 20—Christ is represented as saying to one of the

Seven Churches of Asia: " Behold, I stand at the door, and knock." It is not for the one who stands knocking to open the door, but for the One inside.

I heard the knock early in life, and I opened the door, and the Holy Spirit, the Comforter, whom Christ said He would send, came in. And that Holy Spirit has helped me to live the life I never could have lived without His help.

Jim must have refused that help. I said to the One who knocked and pleaded, saying, " May I come in ? " " Yes, Lord, come in and take full possession. Thou hast given Thyself for me, help me to give myself to Thee." I said yes ; Jim must have said no. The yes and the no makes the difference.

This story is in keeping with the one entitled : " The result of early choice." But that is Dr. Newton's. This is mine. And I have printed it with the idea that many who read it may be induced to say yes, and not no.

Those who have not yet admitted the Holy Spirit have got a Friend at the door.

But will He prove a friend indeed ?
He will—the very friend you need ;
The Man of Nazareth, 'tis He,
With garments dyed at Calvary.

Evangelistic Service.

The Evangelistic work of the Connexion has not been carried out entirely by ministers set aside specially for the work, and devoting their whole time to it, but to some extent by others who have been able to give occasional short periods to the work. This perhaps obtained more in the past than at present. I responded on several occasions to appeals of this kind which were made by the Evangelistic Committee.

The following report of a mission extending over three weeks, which I conducted at Barnoldswick, was sent to the magazine :—

Barnoldswick.

It affords us much pleasure in reporting to the magazine the good work that has been going on here. For some time back the Church has been trying to live very near to God, and earnestly praying for an out-pouring of the Holy Spirit ; and we are happy to say, that the Lord has answered our prayers in a way which exceeded our expectations. It was the unanimous opinion that we ought to hold special services. Several had already professed to find peace in Jesus ; and we believed that God was about to accomplish a mighty work. About this time, October 14th, 1877, Bro. Lee, of Westhoughton, was invited to preach our Chapel Anniversary Sermons, which he kindly consented to do ; and such was the effect of his preaching on this occasion that the church came at once to the conclusion that he was just the man to labour among us. We at once applied to the Evangelistic Secretary, informing him of the

D

About six months after the above date I was requested
by the Evangelistic Committee to come out as one of our
Connexional Evangelists. This splendid meeting at our
own church, and my experience at Barnoldswick, led me
to look upon the call as coming from God, and during the
six years I spent as one of our Connexional Evangelists I
had the opportunity of visiting many of our churches and
many of our people in their homes ; also of praying with
the sick and dying.

The greater part of my time was spent in the Wigan
District, and for two years I was stationed at Stubshaw
Cross.

Our Chapel at Stubshaw Cross, Ashton-in-Makerfield,
had been let to the Welsh Methodists for two years, the
Church and School being in a very low way, but when the
lease expired, Wigan Circuit, as well as the Connexional
Committee, decided to give Stubshaw Cross another trial,
and I was requested to go and live there.   On Sunday,
October 29th, 1882, the Chapel was re-opened. We had a good
congregation on the Sunday, with friends from Golborne,
Brynn, Platt Bridge, and Ince. This gave us a good start
and made a good impression in the neighbourhood.   We
had a Preaching Service every night during the week, and the
School was opened on the following Sunday.   There were
several who had attended before it was closed who came
and were ready to do what they could in the school.   Mrs.
Lee became the teacher of the Young Ladies' Class.   I had
for a time to act as superintendent of the school, teacher of
a Young Men's Class, taking almost all the Preaching
Services, and almost all the addresses in the school.   I read
all John Ashworth's Strange Tales.   These I interspersed

with Bible subjects for a ten minutes' address. We had our Temperance and Band of Hope Meetings. It was very encouraging to see the Church and School prosper.

It was while we were at Stubshaw Cross I sent in my resignation to the Evangelistic Committee, and commenced our present business in Wigan, having by the blessing of God built up a fairly good Church and School. My wife and I continued for twelve months travelling from Wigan to Stubshaw Cross, at least every alternate Sunday, to assist in the school and the public services.

The old Chapel was taken down in 1908, and a new and much larger one was built on the site. I have kept up my visits ever since, having preaching appointments on every plan, and as often as convenient speaking to teachers and scholars in the open school. At the present time there is a good Church, Congregation and Sunday School, and it is a great joy to us in our old age, that is, my wife and I, to think that we have been helpful in saving both Church and School.

us, picked up two small stones for us, and in ten minutes was down again asking for more backsheesh.

On Thursday we visited several mosques, an old Coptic Church, and were shown a crypt where tradition says Joseph and Mary, with the young child Jesus, rested when they fled into Egypt from the wrath of Herod. In the evening we visited the Mosque of the Howling Dervishes. I won't attempt to describe this service. On Friday we rested, staying in Cairo all day. On Saturday we drove to a place called Heliopolis. The name given in the Bible is On (Gen. xli. 45), and we read that Joseph got his wife from On. It is said that On lay either in or near Goshen, and here there stands a large obelisk 66 feet high which was erected 2,433 B.C. We also visited at the same time the Virgin's tree, under which tradition says Mary rested. After this we drove to the Ostrich Farm, which was a sight worth seeing.

On Sunday, March 1st, we attended the English Church, and heard a sermon from Gen. 45, 20, " For the good of all the land of Egypt is yours."

On Monday we left Cairo for Port Said, by rail 132 miles, through a sandy desert, and for 42 miles we ran along or near to the Suez Canal. Arriving at Port Said, we met the Palestine Party, 11 besides our conductor, four ladies and seven gentlemen. We sailed from Port Said to Beyrout and had to undergo a 48 hours' quarantine. We had very good weather, and the sight of the town of Beyrout and the snow clad hills of Lebanon was almost a perfect picture.

On account of the quarantine, a change was made in our programme. We should have commenced the Palestine tour from Jaffa and landed at Beyrout, but now we commence from Beyrout and land at Jaffa. We landed at Beyrout on Sunday, March 8th. On Monday we mounted the horses, and reached Damascus the following Friday.

On Saturday the whole party with our dragoman drove through Damascus, visiting the place where St. Paul was converted ; the house of Judas in the street called Straight ; the house of Ananias ; and the place where Paul was let down in the basket through a window and escaped. On Sunday, March 15th, we attended service at the English Church, and had a little conversation with the clergyman, who told us that their work was amongst the Jews. The English Consul read the lessons at the service. In the afternoon we went outside the city to an elevated spot, and had the pleasure of seeing Damascus and its surroundings to advantage. Damascus is noted for apricot trees, and just now they were white with bloom.

We left this old and interesting city on Monday morning, March 16th, and at night encamped not very far from Mount Hermon. It is supposed by many that the transfiguration of Christ took place here. On Tuesday we were on the road soon after six o'clock, having a long ride and a very bad road before us. Tents were pitched for the night at Banias near Dan, or Ceserea Philippi. We have now entered Palestine. Here is the source of the Jordan. Here Jesus asked His disciples saying " Whom do men say that I the Son of Man am ? " Here it was that Peter made his celebrated confession of Christ, declaring that he was the Son of God. On Wednesday we rode a considerable time along the Jordan Valley, and camped at night near the

Waters of Merom, a lake four and a half miles long and three and a half miles wide, through which the Jordan flows. On Thursday we camped at the Sea of Galilee, near the ruins of Bethsaida. During the day we rode through Rothchild's new colony. The houses are built of stone. He is making good roads, and has planted thousands of fruit trees. We camped two nights by the Sea of Galilee, the second night near Tiberias, so we had the pleasure of spending one full day on and about this very interesting sea or lake, where Christ spent so much of His time and worked many of His miracles. There are a few small boats kept at Tiberias. One of these was engaged and we sailed to Capernaum, and for some time walked amongst the ruins. Chorazin was also pointed out to us. Jesus said that Capernaum was " exalted to heaven." This refers particularly to the fact that Jesus spent so much of His time there. It was a great privilege to be permitted to hear Him preach, and see the miracles that He performed. This seemed to bring heaven very near them; it raised them as it were to its very gate; it would have been easy for them to have stepped in. But the people did not prize their blessings, and so they were taken from them, and they sank as low among cities as they had formerly been exalted. The words of Christ were wonderfully fulfilled. In the wars between the Jews and the Romans, these cities were utterly destroyed, and they have remained so ever since.

We left the Lake of Galilee on Saturday morning, March 21st, for Nazareth, passing very near the Mount of Beatitudes, where Christ preached the Sermon on the Mount. After a four hours' ride we lunched at Cana of Galilee, where Jesus turned water into wine. We approached Nazareth

by one of the hills that surround the town, where we got a
good view of the country. From this point we could see
Mount Carmel and the Mountains of Gilboa, and the Plains
of Jezreel. Nain and Endor were also pointed out to us.
We camped two nights at Nazareth, and had the pleasure
of spending one Sunday in the place where Jesus was
brought up, and where he lived until he was 30 years of age.
Early on Sunday morning I ascended one of the hills alone,
for I felt that I wanted to be alone for a little time in such
a place. I thought of the boyhood days of Christ, and of
the many times he might have ascended the same hill At
eleven o'clock we attended the English Church at Nazareth,
and heard a good sermon on "The Building of the Taber-
nacle." Later in the day we visited the supposed house
of Joseph, and also his workshop. We left Nazareth on
Monday morning, March 23rd, and camped at night at
Jenin. During the day we passed the villages of Nain,
Endor, Shunem and Jezreel. We also crossed the plain of
Esdraelon, going a little out of our way to see the Fountain
of Gideon and the place where Naboth's vineyard was.
On Tuesday morning it began to rain. We had not seen
much Palestine rain up to this date. Our conductor tried
to give us an idea what it was like, and when we had been
on the road a few hours it rained and hailed and blew. The
horses would not face it, but turned round and stood still
until the storm was over. This occurred several times during
the day. When we reached Shechem we were wet through.
That night instead of pitching our tents we put up at a
convent.

Shechem is delightfully situated. It lies in the beautiful
valley that runs between Mounts Ebal and Gerizim. This

is a remarkably fertile valley, sparkling with fountains and streams of water. The streets of the city are narrow and vaulted over, and in the rainy season it is difficult to pass along many of them on account of the streams of water which rush over the pavement with deafening roar. The houses are of stone, resembling in style and general appearance those of Jerusalem The city in its general aspect strikes one as more remarkable for its gloom and filth than any other in Palestine. Soap, indeed, is one of the staple productions of the place ; but then this is made for exportation, and not for home use. The population is about 8,000. Abraham and Jacob dwelt here for a short time. Here all Israel assembled in the time of Joshua. After the death of Solomon, Rehoboam and Jeroboam met here, and the result was the division of the kingdom, Shechem being made the seat of the new government under Jeroboam. The day following we camped at Bethel, about nine hours' ride from Shechem. We arrived late, and the camps were late, and it was eleven o'clock before we got dinner, and twelve o'clock before we retired. On the whole the day had been very interesting. We passed between Shechem and Bethel, Jacob's Well, Joseph's Tomb, and Shiloh, where Eli and Samuel lived, and where Hannah came yearly to sacrifice, bringing with her the little coat for her boy Samuel.

Bethel would long be remembered by Jacob, for it was here after a long journey he slept with a stone for a pillow, and dreamed, and saw a ladder reaching from earth to heaven, and angels ascending and descending upon it. Our position after all was much better than his, for we had a good bed and a tent to cover us.

Bethel is now a poor village on a hill, with wretched huts,

and about 500 inhabitants. Our next ride was from Bethel to Jericho. The day was very fine, but the road was very bad, so much so that we had to get down from our horses several times and lead them over the rocks. During the day we passed through the wilderness of Judea, where John the Baptist spent much of his time. We reached Jericho in the afternoon, and standing upon the ruins of old Jericho we got a good view of the country.

From here we could see the Dead Sea, and the Jordan, the hills of Moab, and Mount Nebo, where Moses stood when God allowed him to see the promised land. One of our party recited a few verses of Mrs. Alexander's poem on the grave of Moses :—

> By Nebo's lonely mountains,
> On this side Jordan's wave,
> In a vale in the land of Moab,
> There lies a lonely grave.
> And no man knows that sepulchre,
> And no man saw it e'er,
> For the fingers of God upturned the sod
> And laid the dead man there.

We camped two nights at Jericho, and on Friday morning we rode down to the Dead Sea. According to the most reliable measurements, the sea is 46 miles long and 9½ miles wide. It lies 1,300 feet below the level of the Mediterranean, and is the most depressed sheet of water in the world. Into this lake the waters of the Jordan empty themselves and are lost. We next rode along the Jordan Valley to what is called the Pilgrim's Bathing Place, about an hour's journey from the Dead Sea. Here we had lunch,

as we looked at this large stone we thought of the women who went to the tomb of Christ saying " Who will roll us away the stone ? " In the afternoon of the same day we drove to Bethlehem, about six miles from Jerusalem, and saw the place where Christ was born, and the shepherds' field. While standing upon a housetop, we had pointed out to us the Cave of Adullam. It was from this cave that David's mighty men, breaking through the garrison of the Philistines, went to Bethlehem to satisfy the desire of their chief, when he cried, " Oh, that one would give me drink of the waters of the well of Bethlehem, which is by the gate." We went to this well and drank of the water. Bethlehem and its Bible associations are very interesting. After the birth of Benjamin, Rachel died, and Jacob buried her in the way to Ephrath, which is Bethlehem. We think of the return of Naomi with Ruth, and of Ruth's marriage to Boaz. We think of Ruth as the mother of Obed, of Obed, the father of Jesse, the father of David, of David the shepherd boy, also the anointing of David by Samuel, and many other interesting events.

On Good Friday, April 3rd, the most interesting places were Gethsemane, Mount of Olives, and Calvary. We had a service on Calvary in the afternoon, conducted by three Church Missionaries, and a very precious time we had. My wife and I spent two hours on Calvary in the morning.

Saturday being the best day to visit the Mosque of Omar, and this being one of the most interesting places in Jerusalem, we gave most of the day to this visit. This Mosque stands where Solomon's Temple formerly stood. Before we were allowed to enter we had to put on slippers over our boots ; these are provided for visitors, but they have to be paid for. This Mosque is believed to stand on the top of Mount Moriah, on which Abraham offered up his son Isaac. In the centre of the Mosque, directly under the dome, is a great mass of rock, which is said to have been the top of Mount Moriah. This rock stands about six feet above the floor of the Mosque. It is irregular in form, a mass of about fifty feet by forty. I won't attempt to describe the building—that rock was the most interesting to me.

On Easter Sunday we went to the Church on Mount Zion, and once more to Calvary, and before leaving Jerusalem I went on the house top with my field glass to have for the last time a general view of the city and its surroundings. Right in front the Mount of Olives—just below the Mount, the Garden of Gethsemane, then the Mosque of Omar, then the Church of the Holy Sepulchre, to my right Mount Zion, to my left Calvary, and in the distance Mizpeh, where Samuel judged the people.

On Monday morning, April 6th, we left Jerusalem by carriage for Jaffa. After five hours' drive, we came to Ramleh, went up the Tower, and got a splendid view of the Plain of Sharon Lydda and other places. We arrived at Jaffa about six o'clock. For a considerable time before landing we were surrounded with beautiful orchards and groves of olive trees, oranges, lemons, citrons, and apricots, which make the country look one great garden. We spent one night here, and on Tuesday morning went to see the house of Simon the tanner, where Peter had a vision.

We sailed from Jaffa on Tuesday night for Port Said, from Port Said to Alexandria, from Alexandria to Pireus,

E

and then by carriage to Athens, where we spent seven days visiting numerous places and objects of historical interest, including the Acropolis, with the Parthenon, Temple of Victory and Mars Hill, where Paul once stood and addressed the admiring men of Athens. I will only just refer to the other places we visited on our homeward journey. From Athens we sailed to Constantinople, where we spent seven days; from Constantinople we sailed to Brindisi. Then by train to Naples, where we spent two days, and from here we visited Pompeii and Puteoli, where Paul landed when he was sent as a prisoner to Rome. Our next run was from Naples to Rome, where we spent two days visiting St. Peter's and the Vatican, the Forum, and the Colosseum. We had a drive along the Appian Way, visited the Catacombs and then we drove to the place where Paul was beheaded. We left Rome on the 9th of May for Florence, where we spent one day. Savonarola preached here, and here he was executed and afterwards burned. Our next run was to Venice, where we spent two nights and one day. Venice may be called the water city, built on piles, having 150 canals, and connected by 378 bridges.

Leaving Venice, we proceeded to Milan, then to Lucerne, where we spent three days; from Lucerne to Ostend, from Ostend to Dover, from Dover to London, and from London to Wigan, arriving home on the 20th of May, having been from home 14 weeks. This I look upon as the tour of my life, which has been very helpful to me in my ministry.

I have used the following story when giving my Palestine Lecture :—

In a village in Yorkshire, lived two men who were cloth manufacturers. One was named Walsh, and the other Stetson. Walsh was an unbeliever. It was a favourite opinion of his that the Bible was " all made up." He could never believe that it was written where it professed to be, and by the men said to have written it. But Stetson was an earnest Christian.

Walsh was part owner of a factory, and one year he had set his heart on making a very large and fine piece of cloth. He took great pains with the carding, spinning, dyeing, weaving, and finishing of it. In the process of manufacture, it was one day stretched out on the tenter-hooks to dry. It made a fine show, and he felt very proud of it. The next morning he arose early to work at it ; to his amazement it was gone. Some one had stolen it during the night.

After weeks of anxiety and suspense, a piece of cloth, answering the description, was stopped at Manchester awaiting the owner and proof. Away to Manchester went Walsh, as fast as the express train could carry him. There he found many rolls of cloth which had been stolen. They were very much alike. He selected one which he felt satisfied was his. But how could he prove it ? In doubt and perplexity he called on his neighbour Stetson.

" Friend Stetson," said he, " I have found a piece of cloth which I am sure is the one which was stolen from me. But how to prove it is the question. Can you tell me how ? "

" You don't want it unless it's really yours ? "

" Certainly not."

" And you want proof that is plain, simple, and such as will satisfy yourself and everybody ? "

" Precisely so."

" Well, then, take Bible proof."

" Bible proof ! Pray, what is that ? "

" Take your cloth to the tenter-hooks on which it was stretched, and if it be yours, every hook will just fit the hole through which it passed before being taken down. There will be scores of such hooks, and if the hooks and the holes just come together right, no other proof will be wanted that the cloth is yours."

" True. Why didn't I think of this before ? "

Away he went, and, sure enough, every hook came to its little hole, and the cloth was proved to be his. The tenter-hooks were the very best evidence that could be had.

Some days after this, Walsh met his friend again.

" I say, Stetson," said he, " what did you mean, the other day, by calling the tenter-hooks ' Bible proof ' ? I'm sure if I had as good evidence for the Bible as I had for my cloth I never should doubt it again."

" You have the same, only better, for the Bible."

" How so ? "

" Put it on the tenter-hooks. Take the Bible and travel with it ; go to the place where it was made. There you find the Red Sea, the Jordan, the Lake of Galilee, Mount Lebanon, Hermon, Carmel, Tabor, and Gerizim ; there you find the cities of Damascus, Hebron, Tyre, Sidon, and Jerusalem. Every mountain, every river, every sheet of water mentioned in the Bible, is there, just as the Bible speaks of it. Sinai, and the desert, and the Dead Sea are there. The holes and the hooks come together exactly. The best guide-book through that country is the Bible. It must have been written there on the spot, just as your cloth must have been made and stretched on your tenter-hooks. That land is the mould in which the Bible was cast ; and when you bring the land and the book together, they fit to perfection."

Walsh felt the force of this argument, and he gave up his infidelity, and began to read the Bible with an interest he never had felt in it before.

PRESIDENTIAL SERVICE.

I began to attend conferences before I was twenty years old. The first opportunity was in 1863, when the conference was held at Folds Road Church, Bolton. I was only able, however, to get there on the Sunday, but it was a great day to me. I had seen and heard some of the old preachers when they came to preach at Wingates, and others I had heard of whom I wanted both to see and hear. It was on this visit to Folds Road that I saw for the first time Thomas Oxley. He passed away after a life of long and faithful service the following year.

I went to the Warrington Conference in 1864. On this occasion I spent the whole time of the Conference there To do this I had to put in special work down the pit, so as to get ahead and be able to spare the time off. I left enough coal down for my drawer to shift during the two days I was away from my work. I did not attend as a delegate, only as a visitor. Alexander Denovan, of Glasgow, was the President, and Edward Twiss was Secretary. Mr. Denovan preached at the morning service, and there was a Camp Meeting in the afternoon, at which the speakers were James Trickett and Thomas Lush. In the evening there were two speakers in the service, and an incident associated with it has fixed this Conference very definitely in my mind.

Edward Twiss conducted the service, and the speakers were William Sanderson and Jeremiah Halliday. I suppose there was an arrangement as to the time each speaker might take. Halliday spoke first, and he had not quite finished when his time was up He looked at Mr. Twiss, and asked if he could have another five minutes. " No, brother," said he, " your time is up." I suppose Twiss wanted to be fair to Mr. Sanderson. Halliday at once sat down. Mr. Halliday was also one of the speakers on the Monday evening, and his subject was : " how to establish a New Testament Church." When called upon, he repeated the title of his address, and then said : " The best way to establish a New Testament Church is to establish it on New Testament principles." That was all, and then he sat down. Naturally this speech, such as it was, was more talked about than any other. If he had spoken for twenty minutes, probably I should have forgotten all about it, but its brevity and its evident connection with the Sunday night incident, impressed it indelibly on my mind.

The first Conference I attended as a delegate was in 1867, at Oldham, and from that time to the present I do not think I have missed more than five or six of the annual assemblies.

We returned from our Palestine tour on the 20th May, 1896, and at the Conference held at Bingley, in June of that year, I was appointed Vice-President of the Connexion. In 1897, at Warrington, I was elected to the Presidency, and I held the position for two years, being re-elected at Moorside, in 1898. I reprint in this chapter the various Conference addresses I gave during that period, either in full or in summary.

ESSENTIALS OF A SUCCESSFUL CHURCH.

ADDRESS DELIVERED AT WARRINGTON, JUNE, 1897, AT
THE MONDAY EVENING PUBLIC MEETING.

A short time ago a gentleman was preaching in the
open air, on the subject of " Growth in Grace." At the
close a man approached him and said : " Our minister
has been preaching some excellent sermons on that subject,
and I have been trying to grow in grace a long time, but I
find I never succeed." The preacher, pointing to a tree,
said, " Do you see that tree ? " " Yes," was the wondering
reply. " Well, it had to be planted before it could grow.
In like manner you must be rooted and grounded in Christ
before you can begin to grow." The man understood his
meaning, and went away to find Christ ; and soon he was
rooted in Him, and brought forth fruit to His praise. " I
am the vine, " says Christ, " ye are the branches ; he that
abideth in Me, and I in him, the same bringeth forth much
fruit ; for without Me ye can do nothing." The Apostle
Paul, speaking of the new birth, calls it putting off the old
man with his deeds, and putting on the new man. It is
one thing to be made alive, and another to be kept alive.
We are pleased when people join the Church, but if the
Church must be successful every member must be joined
to Jesus Christ. Being joined to Him we have the promise
that the " Peace of God, which passeth all understanding,
shall keep our hearts and minds through Jesus Christ."
As good house-keeping is essential to domestic comfort, so
good heart-keeping is essential to a successful Church.

" There is a spotless robe of Christ's own weaving. Wilt thou not wrap it round thy sin-stained soul ? " How to keep Christ in the heart, and how to glorify Christ in the life, is the two-fold secret of a successful Church. What Christ is, every Christian should strive to be. By contact with Christ we become like Him, and we must always remember God expects us to do our best. " Unto one He gives five talents, to another two, and to another one ; to every man according to his several ability." The man with one talent lost it because he did not use it. A working, loving, lovable Christian Church is the most powerful argument for the Gospel. " By this shall all men know that ye are My disciples, if ye love one another." If we would win sinners to the Saviour, we must make our religion winsome. Ye are My witnesses, saith the Lord. May the Lord help us to be good witnesses for Him ! We thank God that we have received the life which Jesus came to give, but we must remember there is life *and life* for Christ says, " I am come that they might have life, and that they might have it more abundantly." To be successful there must be a oneness of purpose, not seeking our own glory, but the Glory of God ; and if the Glory of God is always before us, we shall do good and be made a blessing to others whether we are in the pulpit or behind the door. What I would like to impress upon all Christians is that we are messengers for God. People in the pew look upon the preacher as a messenger. That is right ; I hope no man will ever enter the pulpit without a message ; but we want to teach our people that he is not the only messenger. All converted people are, or ought to be, message bearers. Keeping that thought before us for a little time we shall see that it comes home to all

Christian teachers in our schools, to choirmasters and members of the choir, for we know from experience that the Gospel can be sung as well as preached. If every Church was so filled with the Spirit of Jesus Christ, and every member had a passion for souls we should be successful all round. All our Sunday Schools should appoint two or four male and female members —call them spiritual overseers if you please—spiritually minded and of good character, whose special duty should be to keep an eye upon the people we have about us, who are not in Church fellowship. These spiritual overseers would watch the working of the Spirit, and take our young people especially by the hand, and help them in their trouble. And I would make it known again and again that these brethren and sisters had been specially appointed, and anyone wishing to speak to them could do so with an eye to helping them to Christ and the Church. I would recommend all young converts to begin early to confess Christ publicly. This will help them to grow and become strong. I pray that we may all help forward the Gospel chariot, and never act as a scotch in the wheel. " They that be wise shall shine as the brightness of the firmament, and they that turn many to righteousness as the stars for ever and ever." God grant that we may be amongst those who have turned many to righteousness !

THE CHURCH AND HER MISSION.

ADDRESS GIVEN AT MOORSIDE, 1898, AT THE MONDAY
EVENING PUBLIC MEETING.

Richard Lee said the word ' Church ' meant an assembly or collective body of Christians. The Church which had the most power with God and the most sympathy with men was the truest Church. He knew there were people who denied them that privilege, and who said they did not belong to the true Church. They were not disposed to quarrel with them, but as a body to show that they belonged to the Apostolic Church. If they were among those who were saving men, they might conclude that they belonged to the true Church. For what did the Church exist ? He believed that it was for educating souls for heaven, for making men like Jesus Christ, for making earth like heaven, and the kingdoms of this world the kingdoms of our God. The command of Christ had ever been " Go, run, preach, heal, work." It was clear that the Free Churches had a great work before them in cleansing the public life of our towns and villages. It was awful to think of the evil flourishing under the very walls of their Churches and Chapels. He had read of a great evangelist who had been the means, in God's hands, of bringing many to Christ. Some time passed away, and the evangelist did not see the fruit of his labours. He, therefore, thought that his work was finished, and said to himself, " If this is so, I have no desire to stay here." About this time he had an important dream, in which he thought he died and went to heaven. He there met with one who had been a dear companion, and who had been in heaven some time. His companion led him by the arm along the golden streets of the New Jerusalem. He saw as he went along that the inhabitants of heaven were all turned to see something coming along, and this led to the evangelist and his friend also turning round. They then saw a golden chariot in which was the King of heaven. As the chariot came opposite where they were stood, the King alighted and led the evangelist to the battlements of heaven, from which they could see what was proceeding upon the earth. As they looked over, the evangelist saw a vast procession of people, all making in one direction. They were all blind-folded and moving on, and those in the front disappeared and were lost. The procession seemed to get no less. " Now," said Jesus Christ, " look round ; you are in heaven. I will leave it to you ; if you prefer to stay you can ; or if you would like to go back and help to save those in the procession, you can go back." The evangelist looked, and saw things as he could not on earth. He decided to go back to try to save the mass of people who were hurrying to destruction. Then he awoke, and found it was all a dream ; but it had taught him an important lesson, and God blessed him in his work. He knew heaven would keep. There was a vast amount of work to be done on earth, and he determined that he would do all he could to save that great procession. The mission of the Church of God was to save these men. The Church being made up of individuals, he would refer to individual effort. He had read a book, written by Dean Farrar, entitled " Darkness and Dawn," in which he referred to a man named Telemachus, who was spending his time in idleness. But at length a voice called him to Rome. He obeyed the voice, and when he arrived in Rome he did not know what his mission was to be. He saw a crowd of people making in one direction ; he followed them, and found they were going to the Colosseum. Telemachus followed the people and took his seat in the Collosseum. In a few moments two gladiators entered the arena. On seeing this, the hero flung himself between the combatants and cried " Forbear." For a moment there was silence as of death ; then the silence was broken by a hiss as if coming from a wilderness of snakes. A loud roar was followed by a shower of stones which killed Telemachus. His deed, however, had become a deed which awoke the world, for in the year 423, one of the Roman Emperors decreed that this practice should stop, and it did so. Telemachus gave his life for his mission ; he died for Christ, and in doing so saved hundreds of lives. They might have to suffer, but if it was their mission they should be willing. To reach and win the multitudes outside the Church required more love. There were those who were hungering for love, which would do them more good than bread. If these people were shown that they loved them, he thought they would be more successful in their work than they were. If the mission of Christ was known, the mission of the Church was easily ascertained, for whatever His was, that was the mission of the Church His mission was to seek the lost. He came to soothe human pain and to turn the human race into the pathway of heaven. He was a great believer in individual effort. It was not necessary that they should all preach in pulpits, but it was necessary that they should preach in some way. A good life was never out of season. He who would be successful in saving souls must earnestly wish for their salvation. He believed Demosthenes had a great love for his country, and having that love, he stirred the hearts of the people. They might also stir the hearts of the people by their love of Christ. When they were working in God's great vineyard, they must remember that they were working not for time, but for eternity. He who converted a sinner from the error of his ways, saved a soul from death. Voltaire said he was tired of hearing that it took twelve men to establish Christianity, and he would show that one man could destroy it. Voltaire was dead, and almost forgotten, but Christ was King and reigned, and should reign. It was their duty to tell it out among the nations that the Lord was King, and to spare no effort to tell the news that the King of Glory was the King of Peace.

CONFERENCE AT MOORSIDE, 1898.

THE RETIRING PRESIDENT'S ADDRESS.

Dear Brethren, twelve months ago, when Brother Brimelow vacated the chair, and introduced me to it he said he trusted I should have health for the discharge of my duties, which would be arduous, but which would no doubt afford me both satisfaction and pleasure. So far as the hard work was concerned I was not afraid, and yet I accepted the office of President with fear and trembling, because I felt the position to be a very responsible one. I wish now to thank every member of the Connexional Committee, and every member of this Confer-

ence for their kindness and Christian forbearance. I wish
also to acknowledge the kindness of my friends in Wigan
Circuit in liberating me from Sunday appointments during
my year of office ; also the kindness of all the Churches I
have visited. Many of these have been a considerable
distance from home, and arrangements were made for me to
spend several days in their districts. Will you please excuse
a personal reference. I have been engaged almost every
Sunday and much in the week time. During my year of
office I have visited Sunderland, Bebside, Prescot, Dewsbury,
Elizabeth-street, Tetlow-street, and Chatham Place, Liverpool ; Noble-street, High-street, Chalfont-street, and Folds-
road, Bolton ; Roe Green, Lowton, Urmston, Cleckheaton,
Barrowford, Southport, Westhoughton, Nelson, Farn-
worth, Shildon, Burnley, Thornhill Lees, Pendleton, Bing-
ham, Haslington, Loughborough, Oldham, Moorside, Bingley, Bristol, Ramsey (I.O.M.), Stockton Heath and Crewe.
I have preached 115 times, delivered my Palestine lecture
25 times, and given 30 Sunday School ,Christian Endeavour,
and Band of Hope addresses, making a total of 170. The
wish or prayer of the ex-president that I might have health
for the discharge of my duties has been answered. I have
been able to keep all my engagements with the Churches,
for which in the presence of you all I now thank God, not
only for good health but for all His mercies. I am sure we
are all sorry we have to report a small decrease ; but so far
as our Churches are concerned, I believe there never was a
time when they were better organised and when our people
were so much disposed to seek God's glory. May all our
Churches have a baptism of the Holy Ghost and a deepening
of spiritual life !

We can only be kept healthy and do aggressive work by retaining the missionary spirit. It is not so much great talents that God blesses as great likeness to Jesus, who says " My meat is to do the will of Him that sent Me." Are we not His followers. Shall we be idle when the work so loudly calls for service ? As Lady H. Somerset says, " We shall never climb to heaven by making it our life-long business to save ourselves. The motive is too selfish. The motto of the true Christian is all for each, and each for all, and in trying to realise this we acquire a heart at leisure from itself and in no other way." Our Ministers' Education Scheme is a step in the right direction, our preaching staff having been increased from it. And we pray that God will lay His hand upon the young men in our Churches and make them willing to give themselves to His Service. I would advise all our Churches to join the Free Church Councils, believing that all the Free Churches can heartily co-operate with one another for the advancement of the Kingdom of Christ. Seeing there is so much sin and suffering through drink, let us pay special attention to our Bands of Hope. We have been, and are still, noted for the number of our ministers and members who are total abstainers. In trying to destroy this great monster of intemperance we are doing God's work. Never be afraid to denounce sin in its dark and dreadful features. It needs to be denounced. Let us in this respect plough deep that the good seed may not wither. The subject of leakage has been discussed in the *Methodist Times*. I hope many of our people have read those essays, and as a Connexion I hope that we shall profit by them. As we read the Gospels we find that Christ spent much of His time in training the twelve. The world teaches men that they must seek to be great. Christ taught that His disciples must be little ; that in honour they must prefer one another ; that they are not to be puffed up, not to harbour feelings of envy, but be full of meekness and gentleness and lowliness of heart. A great painter, who was requested to paint Alexander the Great, so as to give a perfect likeness of the Macedonian conqueror, felt a difficulty. Alexander, in his wars, had been struck by a sword, and across his forehead was an immense scar. The painter said : " If I retain the scar, it will be an offence to the admirers of the monarch ; and if I omit it, it will fail to be a perfect likeness. What shall I do ? " He hit upon a happy expedient ; he represented the Emperor leaning on his elbow with his forefinger upon his brow, accidentally as it seemed, to cover the scar upon his forehead Brethren, let us always represent each other with the finger of charity upon the scar, instead of representing the scar deeper and blacker than it really is. I was struck the other day with what may be called the certainties of the Bible. The Bible worthies, being built upon the rock, could speak with certainty. Moses could say to the people " The eternal God is thy refuge, and underneath thee are the everlasting arms."

The Hebrew worthies could say " Our God whom we serve is able to deliver us from the burning fiery furnace, and He will deliver us out of thy hand, O king." David says : " I will bless the Lord at all times, His praise shall continually be in my mouth. My soul shall make her boast in the Lord, the humble shall hear thereof and be glad. O magnify the Lord with me, and let us exalt His name together." Stephen, being full of the Holy Ghost, said he saw the glory of God, and Jesus standing at the right hand

F

of God. It was Paul's faith in God, and being built upon the rock, that kept him up. "Troubled," says he, "on every side, yet not distressed; perplexed, but not in despair; persecuted, but not forsaken; cast down, but not destroyed." There was what might be called a seven-stranded rope at work, doing its utmost to pull Paul from the Rock and separate him from the love of Christ, viz., tribulation, distress, persecution, famine, nakedness, peril, and the sword. All are here in full force, and with what result? Why, when near the end of his life he says "For me to live is Christ, and to die is gain." And when almost in view of the sword he said—" I am now ready to be offered; I have fought a good fight, I have finished my course, I have kept the faith; henceforth there is laid up for me a crown of righteousness, which the Lord, the righteous Judge, shall give to me at that day. And not to me only, but unto all them also that love His appearing." What was the secret of the great and useful life of Mr. Gladstone? We have been told that he went from communion with God to a Cabinet Meeting. Contact with God in that was his strength. His simple child-like faith has been spoken of. What does it mean? The simple faith of a child? That seems an easy thing when it is a child that has to cherish the faith. But here is a giant in intellect with a child-like faith. Nothing too great or small for Gladstone to take to God. It was his deep religious convictions which called forth such a universal feeling of veneration and affection. A well-built life is just the laying up of one grace and good deed upon another; of faith, and patience, and temperance, and benevolence, and courage, and self-denial, and brotherly love. It is growing in grace. It is the sacred architecture of the Holy Spirit.

We are God's building. When a penitent soul has committed itself to Jesus, and the new heart, the new principle, and the new purpose have come to it through conversion, then on this foundation what a beautiful and effective life may be built! My last words shall be: "Jesus Christ the author and finisher of our faith. Jesus Christ, God revealed to forgive and to save. Jesus Christ, your Lover and your Friend. Jesus Christ, your Guide and your Judge. Jesus Christ, your Eternal Reward." "Other foundations can no man lay than that which is laid, which is Jesus Christ."

SCATTERING AND WITH-HOLDING.

SUMMARY OF ADDRESS AT THE PUBLIC MEETING, MONDAY
EVENING, SALEM CHURCH, NELSON,
1899 CONFERENCE.

Scattering we find on every farm, in every business, and in every school. The farmer will tell you if the land be starved the crop will be starved. The business man will tell you that he must be liberal in his outlay, or he will be short in his income. The schoolmaster will tell you the way to increase is to give out. The very exercise of giving carries with it a blessing, by breaking up selfishness. He who never gives anything away is to be pitied. A man gives away £50 in Christ's name and for Christ's sake. He says: The money may be mine, but I myself am not my own. How then can anything be mine? I am God's steward and

I am responsible to Him. I may have given society an equivalent for the £50, and in that sense it is mine. But the strength, the skill, and the knowledge by which I gained it are God's gifts. When giving is done in that spirit, it is a holy thank-offering. So to give is to scatter and to increase. Such a man increases all round, the heavens become brighter, his cup of comfort is sweetened, he walks on a greener earth, he looks up to God through a bluer sky. "Give, and it shall be given unto you, good measure, pressed down, shaken together, and running over." "The liberal soul shall be made fat, and he that watereth shall be watered himself." You may think it a dangerous doctrine to preach that if a man gives away a sovereign he may get two or ten. If a man gives in that spirit he will be disappointed. It is when a man gives, free from all self-consciousness, that he gets the blessing. No man works for God for nothing. His water is often turned into wine. Many a man has made a vow to God, and while it has been kept all has gone right, but when broken all has gone wrong. Selfishness is suicidal. Selfishness lives in gloom and injects poison into every stream of life. God is against the selfish heart. The selfish man may accumulate and be what the world calls rich, but there is no enjoyment in it. The sun, and rain, and the beautiful flowers, are all against the selfish man. It is strange that men by grasping should lose, but it is so. The selfish man's success is turned to failure and disappointment. This is not a temporary law, it is a moral principle. Remember the words of the Lord Jesus, how He said "It is more blessed to give than to receive." I hope we have learned that lesson. To the non-christian these things may sound very foolish. By getting out of self we do ourselves the greatest service. Let there be self-forgetfulness, self-crucifixion, and then there will be blessing until there is not room to contain it. Scatter liberally with a right motive, and you shall have a rich harvest. To the young people present I would say : Be true, be noble, be self-oblivious, live a holy life, and may the Great Father gather you to His heart and bless you evermore. This scattering and with-holding cuts many ways. A man cannot be good without enriching his own soul. Whatever we do in the way of mercy does not terminate upon the object to which it is addressed, but comes back to the soul itself, enlarging its capacity and refining its whole nature. On the other hand, the cruel man is always inflicting trouble upon himself ; when he thinks he is troubling others he is in reality thrust-ing the iron into his own soul. This is the dispensation under which they live. " Whatsoever a man soweth that shall he also reap."

CONFERENCE AT SALEM CHURCH, NELSON, 1899.

THE RETIRING PRESIDENT'S ADDRESS

I desire to thank the General Secretary, Mr. F. Wilkinson, for the great assistance he has given me during my two years of office. I feel that you honoured me two years ago by appointing me to the Presidential chair. I came to it in fear and trembling, but you have helped me in many ways. I wish to thank the Churches, those I have visited for the way they have received me, and all those I have not been able to visit for their kind forbearance. I had no idea twelve months ago that I should be elected for a second year. During my first year of office, I was often from home visiting Churches in many parts of our Connexion. During the past year I have not made many long journeys, but I have been fully engaged, and in addition to my Sunday appointments, I have been able to do some little mission work during the year. We are not able to report an increase, but, I regret to say, a decrease. Still, all things considered, I think our Churches were never stronger. They are coming more into line, have a better Connexional spirit, and are better organized. We never stood better with the other Churches than we do to-day. Many of our Churches have joined the Free Church Councils, and I would advise others to do the same.

For the first time in the history of the Free Churches, there was a meeting of Free Church Presidents, held in the City Temple, London, on the 1st of December last year, when I had the honour to represent you.

We glory in our freedom, and we have a right to glory. To those who know how to appreciate it, and how to use it, it is a very great blessing, but when Churches abuse it, it becomes a curse. On behalf of the Connexional Committee I say with Paul, " We are jealous over you with a Godly jealously." We are always pleased to hear of good work done for God.

We hear a good deal about Apostolic Succession. Dr. Parker says :—" He who inherits the Apostolic spirit, and lovingly undertakes Apostolic work, is in the Apostolic Succession. Apostolicity is not an order—it is a spirit.

The Church is an instrument for purifying and perfecting human souls. Like the Sabbath it was made for man, and the true test of its worth is the measure in which it serves to make men good and useful. What sort of characters is the Church forming ? is a question we have a right to ask." What are the children like that the Churches are bringing up ? For what does the Church exist ? Why did Christ die ? That He might bring us to God.

> He died that we might be forgiven,
> He died to make us good.

We propose asking all our members to be total abstainers from all intoxicating liquors, and not to be shareholders in breweries or drinking clubs. It has been our boast in the past that a very large percentage of our ministers and members were total abstainers. When other Churches kept their doors closed against the seven men of Preston and early Temperance advocates, our people at Bolton, Warrington, Wigan, Westhoughton, and elsewhere, allowed them the use of their Chapels and schools for public meetings. Have we lowered our standard ? I hope not. In a book just published, entitled "The Temperance Problem and Social Reform," by Messrs. Rowntree & Sherwell, the writers state that among the obstacles that stand in the way of any comprehensive measure of Temperance reform, the most serious is to be found in the magnitude of the vested interest in the maintenance of the traffic. What is the extent of the vested interest ? Quoting from the Brewers' Almanac for 1898, it is there given at £230,000,000. Notice the social position of many of the shareholders in five large Brewery Companies. In Guinness and Company, women are the most numerous, then come Peers, titled persons, and doctors. In this company there are 178 persons bearing the title of Rev.; including Bishops, Deans, Archdeacons, and Canons. In four other smaller companies there are 133 persons designated Rev., making a total of 311 shareholders ministers of the Gospel. I hope we as a body are clear of this traffic. How can the Kingdom of God come on the earth while those who profess to be building with one hand are pulling down with the other ?

You would notice from the general report that the book room is now prepared to supply our Churches with Temperance Pledge Cards and Pledge Books, and we suggest that pledge cards should be kept on hand in our Churches and schools, and as often as convenient the people should be urged to sign the pledge. The late Miss Willard, speaking at a great meeting during the liquor war in America, referred to what one of the opponents had said :—" We are bound to win," said he. " We have the drinking men on our side. We have money on our side, and money is power, and don't forget it." Miss Willard replied, " We have the sober men on our side. We have the women on our side, we have God on our side, and God is a power, and don't forget it." Yes, God is on our side ; the Bible is on our side ; the necessities of humanity are all on our side, and we call upon all the delegates to this Conference, and all the members of the Independent Methodist Churches everywhere, in the name of Christ, and in the name of everything humanizing and up-lifting, to join in the effort to bring dear old England out of the wilderness of drunkenness.

ECUMENICAL AND
OTHER CONFERENCE ADDRESSES.

The Conference of 1910 appointed myself and Mr. John Battersby to represent our Churches at the Ecumenical Conference, held at Toronto, Canada, in October, 1911. I was invited to give one of the ten-minute addresses, and I spoke as follows :—

THE PRIESTHOOD OF THE PEOPLE.

The Apostle Peter, writing to the Churches of Asia Minor— not to any one order, such as ministers, deacons, or evangelists, but to the ordinary members, Jews and Gentiles, male and female—speaks of them as a royal priesthood.

For he says : " Ye also, as lively stones, are built up a spiritual house, an holy priesthood, to offer up spiritual sacrifices, acceptable to God by Jesus Christ." (1 Peter 2: 5).

When Peter wrote these words it is quite evident that he had his eye upon the great temple at Jerusalem, which was esteemed and honoured by the whole Jewish race. He not only thought of the building as a whole, but also the separate stones, each having passed under the builder's eye. And then, by a bold venture of the imagination, he thought of these stones as endued with life.

Notice the apparent incongruity; for what is so dead as a stone? Yet Peter speaks of *lively* stones. Let us try and find out what is in his mind.

Is it not this, think you, that if the stones of the temple could really know what they were, and the purpose they served, how together they constituted the most magnificent building ever reared in their beloved country, and reared for the highest purposes, viz: the worship of the Lord Jehovah; then they would rejoice in the honour done to them in bringing them from the quarry and shaping them and fashioning them and devoting them to such noble use?

Then thinking of a living temple made of men and women, he says, "Ye also, as lively stones, are built up a spiritual house." And if we truly realise that, as lively stones, we are a part of Christ's world wide spiritual temple, even His Church, then we shall value our place at the very highest and do our utmost to adorn it.

The Church is composed of Christ's disciples: "a royal priesthood, an holy nation, a peculiar people;" and it embraces all His followers, however numerous or scattered, or separated into distinct congregations.

Spiritual sacrifices which Christians are to offer are: their bodies, souls, affections, prayers, praises, alms, and other duties.

Dr. Parker, speaking of the ministry and the priesthood, says we are all ministers; there are speaking ministers, and giving ministers, and sick-visiting ministers, and quiet,

sympathetic ministers.   We are all the Lord's prophets, but
are only in the apostolic succession so long as we adhere to
the apostolic spirit.   Apostolicity is not an order, but a
spirit.

We are all the Lord's priests, but we are only in the holy
royal priesthood so long as we are offering spiritual sacrifices : doing kind deeds for Christ.   Priesthood has no
standing but in holiness and in the sanctification of the will
and heart and the total sacrifice of the man to God ; and
thus we maintain the priesthood of believers. When we read
of the priesthood of the people in the New Testament, and
the sacrifices they are to offer, we must remember it is not
what it was in the old order.   The official priest was dis-
established when the Christian Church was founded, because
no longer did lambs and oxen need to be slain, the time for
such sacrifices having passed away.

The old sacrifice involved the *taking* of life ; the new
Christian sacrifice involves the using of life.   The term
" sacrifice " is often used in a secondary or metaphorical
sense, and applied to the good work of believers—such as,
" To do good and communicate, forget not ; for with such
sacrifices God is well pleased." " I beseech you by the mercies
of God that ye present your bodies a living sacrifice, holy
and acceptable to God, which is your reasonable service."
A service rendered by the reason ; intelligent ; self-dedica-
tion ; the spiritual in opposition to the carnal ; a living
sacrifice, in contrast with the dead victims under thé law.

The priests of the New Testament are simply ordinary
followers of Christ, and the sacrifices they offer are not
material, but spiritual.

But God has said, The blood of goats, the flesh of rams, I will not prize; a contrite heart, an humble thought, are Mine accepted sacrifice.

What are spiritual sacrifices? Every longing and aspiration of the soul after righteousness and loveableness of character is a spiritual sacrifice. Every prayer coming from a true heart, whether offered privately or in association with others. Every kind thought and every kind deed which springs from it; every service, however small, done in Christ's name and for His sake, is a spiritual sacrifice. A cup of water given as Christ desired; the widow's mite bestowed in real charity, is a spiritual sacrifice. The child, moved by pity for the heathen, who puts his penny in a missionary box instead of spending it upon himself, offers a spiritual sacrifice, as well as the missionary who gives his life to the cause. There may be a difference of degree, but the same spirit. The good woman who, sympathising with her neighbour who is unwell and not able to do her own housework, goes in and does her week's washing for her— she is offering a beautiful spiritual sacrifice amid the steam of a washhouse. Every act and every deed that has in it the spirit of Christ is a spiritual sacrifice. The fruit of the Christian spirit is not self-indulgence, but self-sacrifice. A millionaire once said to Lyman Abbott, " A millionaire rarely laughs; we do not get our pleasure from what we possess." We get our pleasure from the service we render. We find our real life not in the things we gain, nor in the things we possess, but in the things we give up. In Africa some Englishmen who went out to shoot lions and elephants spoke to Dr. Livingstone about his self-sacrifice. Livingstone turned to them and said, " Don't you fellows think I can find as much pleasure in doing good to men and women as you do in killing lions and elephants ? " In the spiritual world we grow more upon what we give than upon what we receive.

When Whittier was a little boy of seven, he was taken by his mother to see a girl who had wandered far into sin and was very ill. The boy noticed how his mother addressed her. " My dear," she said, and she gave her food and comfort. In after years, he says, I went out of doors and looked up to the blue sky. I thought that God who lived up there must be as good as my mother. Since then I have never doubted the goodness of God. That was a beautiful spiritual sacrifice offered by Mrs. Whittier which helped her boy to see God through her. He climbed up through the human love of his mother into the divine love of God.

When Telemachus threw himself between the gladiators and cried, " Forbear, in the name of Him who died for men, Christ Jesus, my Lord, I say, forbear ! " that act cost his life, but it saved the gladiators. This spirit of self-sacrifice has done much and is doing much for the world. It freed the slave ; it protected the captive ; it nursed the sick ; it sheltered the orphan, and elevated woman ; where its tidings were believed it cleaned the life and elevated the soul of each individual man.

Harriet Beecher Stowe was a priestess of freedom. The mother of a large family, and a capable housewife, when asked about her book, " Uncle Tom's Cabin," she said, " I did not write it ; God wrote it." The truth is, God helped her and she helped God. She received a letter from one of her sisters telling her of the heartrending events caused by the enforcement of the fugitive slave law. In this letter she said, " Now, Hattie, if I could use a pen as you can I would write something that would make this whole nation feel what an accursed thing slavery is." After reading it to her family she said, " I will write something, I will, if I live." This was the origin of " Uncle Tom's Cabin." From that time onward her life was a beautiful spiritual sacrifice.

Lloyd George, speaking a short time ago at a religious meeting, said, ' Destroy the spirit of religion and the spirit of self-sacrifice, and the country will be turned into a burned-up wilderness."

Find out what God would have you do, and do that little
        well ;
For what is great and what is small, 't is only He can tell.
My residue of days and hours Thine, wholly Thine shall be,
And all my consecrated powers a sacrifice to Thee.

" Unto Him that loved us, and washed us from our sins in His own blood, and hath made us kings and priests unto God and His Father, to Him be glory and dominion for ever and ever. Amen."

CONFERENCE AT BARNOLDSWICK, JUNE, 1911.

THE SUNDAY SCHOOL.

Taking as his subject " The Sunday School and Moral Demands upon it," Richard Lee asked if we could rest satisfied with an acknowledged leakage from our schools of 80 per cent. This question, he said, has troubled us for 40 years since Charles Garrett published his famous address

" Stop the gap." It was 90 per cent then, it is 80 per cent.
now ; but where are the 80 out of every 100 ? Many have
passed the junction and joined the crowd of the ungodly,
the drunkards, the gamblers, and the thieves. What can
we do for them ? We cannot force them into the kingdom.
Converted men and women must take this matter to heart·
Fifteen distinguished men have recently answered three
questions addressed to them by the editor of " The Quiver."
The questions were these : (1) Has the Sunday School failed,
or partially failed, to bring the children to Christ and into
the Church ? (2) Who is responsible for the fact that the
majority of our Sunday School Scholars do not pass into the
Church ? Is it the Sunday School or the Church ? (3)
What practical means do you suggest for improving the
present condition of affairs ? The answers to these questions
are given in the May issue of " The Quiver." In almost
every case the answer to the first question is " Failed," and
to the second " Everybody concerned." As regards the
third—the remedies—the spirit of the answers is that the
real remedy is spiritual revival, a recovery in the school of
the sense of its evangelistic mission. Revival is needed
even more than reform. The severance of the Church and
the schools is schism of the worst character. The school
should be an essential part of the Church, not an appendage.
The very life of the Church is bound up with our work among
the young people. And the life of the nation, its moral and
Christian progress, is vitally bound up with it also. The
remedies suggested are very varied. They include a system
of inspection, more definite Church teaching, and the check-
ing of the spirit of independence and resultant lawlessness.
I consider that the remedy can only come through waiting

Christ made a great promise to His disciples when they asked Him if He would at that time restore again the Kingdom to Israel. He did not give them the answer they expected.

But He said " Ye shall receive power, after that the Holy Ghost is come upon you, and ye shall be witnesses unto Me both in Jerusalem, and in all Judea, and in Samaria, and unto the uttermost *part of the earth.*"

We are called to a mission *and we are entrusted with a message*.

I have copied a few lines from the article in our May magazine, by Rufus Jones.

THE POWER OF CONFESSION.

He says :—I saw a large school once melted with feeling, and my own eyes were filled with tears of joy, as a girl, who had been the leader of the school, rose unexpectedly in a meeting and said : " I have not been living the kind of life I ought to live. It has been really a failure. I am going to begin all over again, and I am going to follow Christ."

That message took the hearts of all present by storm, and many lives were changed as the result.

She had laid upon her a responsibility. If she had not followed the leading of the Spirit, she would have been condemned.

Some of you may be there—you may feel perhaps, just now, that you ought to confess Christ. This may be the time when you ought to rise up and go to Him. God is coming towards you. Though men may go away from God,

God cannot go away from men. The disciples and apostles previous to Pentecost did very little. God, through the Holy Spirit, is saying, "Without Me you can do nothing."

I don't want to say anything that will hurt the quiet, timid Christians. You may be amongst those who are helping others in a quiet way. In some you stimulate the mind. In others you check ambition—in others you elevate the purpose of life. Rather than discourage you, I want to speak a word of comfort. A boy was once asked under whose preaching he was converted. He replied, under nobody's preaching, but under Aunt Mary's practising.

A LEGEND.

A lady who writes in the *Christian Age* tells the following story—or legend : " In a little village it was rumoured one afternoon that an angel was coming, and was going to measure everybody, and the person who reached the required standard would, regardless of rank or position, be made the reigning sovereign of the village. Presently the angel arrived. He was carrying a long rod, which mysteriously became shorter or longer according to the person measured. The rector stepped up first, but before the angel measured him he insisted on the clerical hat, coat and tie being removed, and after placing the rod against him—to the surprise of the rector himself and all his parishoners— passed him by. Then the minister was tested. He was not asked to preach, for it was not the beautiful things that are easily spoken that the angel placed his rod against. But oh ! how disappointed the Chapel folks were when the minister was rejected. Then the church-warden, the deacon, the Sunday School teacher, and the squire—who actually came in his motor, and with his heaps of money felt sure of being made king—were put to the test, but failed to satisfy the angel. Then a big man of business came up. He was chairman of the County Council and a great deal beside. He was always kind and appeared to be friendly with everybody; but when the measuring rod was placed against him he had never appeared so short. It was whispered that his business transactions would not always bear the searching light of day. The ladies of the village were now invited to come forward: Mrs. Rector, Mrs. Minister, Mrs. Deacon, Mrs. District Visitor, etc., but the angel measured them one by one only to reject them. And the villagers began to think there would be neither a king nor a queen chosen. But just at that moment the angel beckoned to a poorlooking, little woman, and she was seen to shake her head in response. The people laughed outright at the very idea of the angel even thinking of measuring a poor dressmaker; one, too, who seldom was seen in public, for it often happened that she was sitting with some poor body who was ill, or comforting some one in trouble. However, the angel insisted upon measuring her, so she very reluctantly came to the fore; and as she did so various thoughts flashed through the minds of the villagers—When Annie's baby was born—When little Flo died—When Grannie was ill. But before anyone could finish giving expression to their thought the little woman was standing beside the angel, and as they stood side by side it was observed how very much alike they were. The people she had lived amongst had only thought of her as a poor, humble, little seamstress. But now they saw her honoured by God and owned as His peculiar treasure, because her life had been consecrated to her Master's service.

The Power of Influence.

Let us each fill in the application for ourselves, and may we each know what it is to be set apart or consecrated to God. A noted preacher once said : I have known a few men and women who have done more to make me believe in God and goodness than all the books I ever read. Their names never get into the newspapers, but their sanctity pervades the air like perfume from the heavenly fields. They walked with God. The Christian mother has her home duties. The Sunday School teacher is , or ought to be, one to whom the young people can look up to. I am not confining myself to any one order of Christian service. We talk about our beautiful churches. Nothing makes beautiful churches like beautiful christians. There is one little word in connection with the Pentecost I want you to notice— *All.* And by that word "all" you must not understand the Apostles only.

I am one of your ministers of 48 years standing. But on that account I claim no more of God's spirit and grace than any other man in the Church may claim. We can each have a filling of the Spirit, which will prepare us for service. I feel my responsibility more than ever. I have 50 years of Christian service behind me. What is the impression ? If, by the help of God, I have made *good* ; I must see that it continues. The life and the word must go together. If, by the help of Christ, I have got to that point when I can be trusted, believed, and looked up to, I must be careful not to betray that trust. And looking at life and service in this way, I feel my responsibility. But I get comfort from the thought that Christ is alive and by my side, always ready to help. And I would rather have one smile from Christ than the applause of the world. To hear the Master say: " Well done, good and faithful servant, thou hast been faithful over a few things, I will make thee ruler over many. Enter thou into the joy of thy Lord."

O, that each in the day
Of His coming may say,
I have fought my way through.
I have finished the work
Thou did'st give me to do.

O, that each from his Lord
May receive the glad word:
" Well and faithfully done.
Enter into My joy,
And sit down on My throne."

LATEST PORTRAIT OF MR. AND MRS. LEE.

MINISTERIAL JUBILEE AND GOLDEN WEDDING CELEBRATIONS.

The following are reprints of reports which were published on the occasions referred to.

MINISTERIAL JUBILEE.

The Church at Kendal Street, Wigan, celebrated the Jubilee of Mr. Lee as a Preacher, on Saturday, January 3rd, 1914. Tea was provided, at which a large number were present.

A Public Meeting followed, held in the Church, where there assembled representatives from the various churches in Wigan and surrounding districts, also from Crewe, Ashton-under-Lyne, Liverpool, St. Helens, Bolton, Horwich, Moorside and Swinton. Others present were: Mr. W. Rigby, President Band of Hope Union; Mr. Murray, Sunday School Union; and Mr. J. Anders, Temperance and Rescue Mission. The Meeting was addressed by Messrs. R. B. Woods, T. Worthington, Wm. Price, T. Martlew, J. Trickett, Councillor G. Hunter, Wm. Murray, and J. A. Johnson, J.P., President of the Wigan Free Church Council. Mr. T. Perry, President Wigan District Churches, presided. Special old Methodist hymns and tunes were sung.

During the evening presentations on behalf of the Kendal Street Church, and district Churches and friends, were made to Mr. and Mrs. Lee : a writing table and book rest, with a suitable inscription upon it, to Mr. Lee, and a beautiful hand-cut rose bowl to Mrs. Lee. The present to Mrs. Lee was subscribed for by the scholars and teachers in the Sunday School. The presentations were made by Mr. Thomas Wragg.

Mr. Lee, on behalf of himself and Mrs. Lee, suitably responded, and at the same time thanked the members and representatives of the Independent Methodist Churches and the various representatives of the other bodies mentioned, for their kind and encouraging words, and for their presents. He stated that he had received a large number of telegrams, letters and postcards of congratulation from representatives of various churches, and also persons in the street, and stated " that he thought he was old and strong enough not to allow all the congratulations to make him vain, but rather tend to make him humble, and help him in his work in the future." He also stated that " he never looked upon preaching as a light matter, but he had often been helped when he thought of what Christ said to those early preachers : ' Lo, I am with you alway.' " His faith in God and the promises of Jesus Christ had been helpful to him all along.

On Sunday afternoon and evening he preached at Dicconson Lane Chapel. It was here he preached his first sermon, as a recognised minister, on January 3rd, 1864. During his fifty years ministry Mr. Lee has preached more than five thousand times, and he made very kindly reference in his address to the great help and encouragement he has always received from Mrs. Lee.

On Sunday, January 11th, Mr. Lee preached morning and evening at Kendal Street, and in the afternoon gave a short address at a musical service given by a Junior Choir from the Independent Methodist Church, Lamberhead Green. The singing at this service was much appreciated.

GOLDEN WEDDING CELEBRATIONS.

A very large gathering of friends from many counties, and from the Isle of Man, assembled in the Kendal Street Independent Methodist Church, Wigan, on March 29th, 1916, to offer their congratulations to Mr. and Mrs. Lee, who were married on March 26th, 1866. Tea was provided in the School room and somewhere near 300 friends sat down to a bountiful repast. After tea, an old friend, Mr. R. B. Woods, presided at the meeting in the Chapel, where a fine programme of musical items was rendered by the Crawford Glee Party. The organ solo by Mr. Knight was greatly enjoyed, and the exquisite rendering of songs and duets were a real, rich treat. The recitations by Mr. Holland, of Bolton, were appreciated.

The Chairman, in offering congratulations in the name of the guests, said they all esteemed the kind and abundant hospitality. They were glad for the arrangement that no personal gifts were desired, but all gifts were to go to the reduction of the debt on the Chapel premises. They all were disposed to give praise to God for His gracious companionship with their friends for 50 years. Success had not narrowed their souls, nor years spoiled them. They admired the sacrifice of Mrs. Lee in making it easy for her husband to prepare and travel and preach the gospel for the whole of their married life. What they all wanted to know was the secret of this long and happy life. They were told it was their contentment. But there was a contentment that was quite unworthy; merely to be satisfied if they could eat comfortably, sleep comfortably, and escape disturbance. The secret seemed to be, happiness had come when not deliberately sought. To seek happiness was almost to miss it. They believed in seeking the happiness of others. They could not keep it out of their own life, as seen by the fine spirit of the employer and employees. They rejoiced that the eventide of Mr. and Mrs. Lee's life was so peaceful. They remembered their liberality to that and all the Churches, their loyalty to the connexion, their hospitality to their ministers, and their constant devotion to every good work. They were glad for the golden influences for good they had brought to all their lives, and wished them all blessings to the end.

> They have lived long;
> They have lived well.

Mr. Lee presented the offerings to Mr. Silson, the President of the Church, amounting to over £60, and in felicitous terms thanked all for their kindness, and rejoiced that so large a number had responded to their invitation.

SELECTED SERMONETTES AND OUTLINES.

Looking over a number of my sermon notes of recent date, and thinking of the good times I have had during the delivery of the same, and knowing that many have been helped and blessed by them, I am strongly moved to print a few sermonettes, trusting that the reading of them may also be helpful to the reader :—

THE PROMISE I MADE TO GOD.

Standing on Mount Calvary, on that never-to-be-forgotten Good Friday Morning, 27 years ago, I thanked God for many things.

I thought of this great gift: that God had given His best to the world; and if I must have God's best, I must give Him my best. And that morning, the day held in commemoration of the Crucifixion of Christ, and there in spirit standing under the Cross, I made God a promise. If spared, I would, by His help, try and help the young folks, not only the boys and girls, but the young men and women. I am anxious to help them over that critical period between 15 and 21.

And during the 27 years I have been trying to fulfil my promise, and I hope the reader will read carefully the Sermonettes printed in this book.

I see things much clearer than I did 60 years ago. I have tried, and am still trying, to simplify the Gospel. Please let me help you into the light, and to Jesus Christ, our best Friend. We cannot live the good life without His help. And He is so willing to help us. But there must be a willingness on our part to receive what He is so willing to give. Salvation is wrapt up in two words—giving and receiving.

When Holman Hunt had finished his great picture, "The Light of the World," one of his critics said he had made a great mistake, not having put a latch on the door. "No," said the artist, "no mistake, the latch is inside." "Behold," says Christ, "I stand at the door and knock." When He has done that He has done all He can. It is not for Him to open the door, but for the one inside. It is for us to lift the latch and say: Come in, Thou Friend of Sinners, come in, and help me to live the good life.

I believe in early conversion. Many years ago a conference was held in New York. Many ministers were present, and it was made known to the meeting that 149 decided for Christ before they were 15 years of age, and many before they were 12. Referring to my own experience, I am pleased to say I never left the Sunday School, signed the Temperance pledge at 12 years of age, accepted Christ as my Saviour, Friend, and Helper, at 14. Commenced to preach at 19. I have been helped and encouraged when I have thought of the words uttered by Jesus after the Resurrection, and just before the Ascension. " Lo, I am with you alway, even unto the end of the world." Every preacher of Christ's gospel has a right to claim that promise· In front of the Church where Philips Brooks ministered for many years stands a bronze statue of the great preacher. His right hand raised, as was his wont, and just behind, a figure of Christ, with His hand resting on the preacher's shoulder, and Christ is represented as saying " Do your best, I am here." If we could always feel that Christ was with us in the pulpit, or as one of the congregation, and saying to us, do your best, I am here, our preaching would never be shallow..

I am in love with Jesus, and for 60 years I have had the privilege of lifting Him up, and I know the people have felt the drawing influence. 'Whatever of life still remains to me, I give it to Him without stint.

Here is the testimony of three noted men : Sir James Simpson, Coleridge, and Wilberforce.

Sir James Simpson, the renowned physician and discover-er of chloroform, was once asked by a lady : " What is the most important discovery you have ever made, Sir James ?" The great man quietly replied : " Madam, the greatest discovery I ever made was that Christ is my Saviour." That is a discovery every one can make. The Cross is still the power of God unto salvation to every believing soul.

Coleridge, the English poet, writing to a young friend, just before his death, said " Health is a great blessing ; wealth, gained by honest industry, is a great blessing ; it is a great blessing to have kind, faithful, loving friends and relatives ; but the greatest and best of all blessings is to be a Christian."

William Wilberforce, when he was on his death bed, said to a dear friend : " Come , let us talk of heaven ; I am very happy, but I never knew what happiness was till I found Christ as my Saviour."

I have met with hundreds of people during the sixty years I have been preaching, who seem to be ignorant of the plan of salvation, and indeed very much in the dark. That such may be helped, I have tried in the sermonettes which follow to simplify the gospel, showing how God works, and what is expected from man. Salvation, when we understand it, is simple—God loves and gives ; the sinner believes and receives.

What must I do to be saved ?

Discover the law and obey it ! Though I cannot explain the mystery of the new birth, I shall receive the benefit of the Spirit's power, and shall get the life. But what is the law ? " And as Moses lifted up the serpent in the wilderness, even so must the Son of man be lifted up : that whosoever believeth, may in Him have eternal life." Here is the law ! Life comes by the Spirit when you believe on the lifted Son of man. Recognise the mystery of the Spirit's operation. Obey the law, and immediately receive the benefit. Just as the man on the lake, who, not understanding the mystery of the coming and going of the wind, yet obeys its laws by lifting his sail so as to catch it, and finds his boat driven across the water ; so you, helpless man, unable to understand the mystery of the Incarnation, or the Atonement, or Regeneration, lift your sail, crown

Christ by trusting Him, and the divine life shall fill your soul.

It is a great mystery! Begin this life; begin right where you are, saying "O Christ, Revealer of God, Redeemer of men, by the mystery of the Passion that I cannot understand, in obedience to the call of Thy love, I trust Thee with my soul."

God help us to see that there is mystery that cannot be explained, though there is also a law that is simple enough for a child; and that when we obey the law, all the forces of God's life in Christ are made ours by the work of the Spirit.

1.—THE BIRTH OF CHRIST.

Luke 2; 11.—*Unto you is born this day a Saviour.*

This is just what the world wanted.

What does a drowning man want? A strong grip.

What does a sinner want? A Saviour.

Christianity is something to be received into the heart or life, if we are to be benefited and helped by it.

The Birth of Christ unites Heaven with Earth, the Divine with the Human, God with Man.

God comes in Christ to live our life as it **was** meant to be lived.

And we are requested to look to Him to learn of Him.

He came to teach us what we never could have learned any other way.

We do well to be grateful for His coming.

We do well to sing Christmas Carols and hymns of praise.

May our praise be shown in a life that will tell upon others.

May you be of those who can say from the heart, He is my Saviour, my Christ, my Lord.

And if you can go so far, you will know something of the joy which the angel spoke of.

Christ was like sunrise in the world.

Let us think of Him under four heads, viz :—The time of His Birth, the place of His Birth, the circumstances of His Birth, and the reasons for His Birth.

1. The time of His birth.

1,923 years since our Lord's Incarnation, which means the act of clothing with flesh, the act of assuming flesh, or taking on a human body and the nature of man.

2. The Place of His Birth.

700 years before His birth the place had been foretold.

The Prophet Micah had said :—" But thou, Bethlehem, Ephratah, though thou be little among the thousands of Judah, yet out of thee shall He come forth unto me that is to be ruler in Israel."

Joseph and Mary, the Parents of Jesus, lived at Nazareth, 80 miles from Bethlehem.

Why did they journey from Nazareth to Bethlehem ?

Augustus Cæser, the Emperor of Rome, sent forth a

decree for enrolling, or making a census, of all the inhabitants of Syria.

And every family had to go up to the city of their fathers.

Joseph and Mary belonged to Bethlehem.

The Emperor of Rome helped to fulfil one of the most important of the Bible prophesies.

3.   The circumstances of His birth.

There were strange contrasts in connection with the Birth of Christ.

The neglect on the one hand, and the attention on the other.

The poverty on the one hand, and the wealth on the other.

Humiliation on the one hand, and glory on the other.

We have clearly set before us the strangely opposing circumstances that marked His birth, or in other words, we see how Christ was born.

4.   Why was Jesus born ?

The angel said that His coming into the world would bring peace on earth and good will towards men.

And at the same time it would bring glory to God in the highest places.

Glory to God in the highest creatures, glory to God in the highest measure.

Christ was born to reveal God's love.

We must not think that God loves us because Christ was born, and suffered, and died.

H

Nor that Jesus was born and suffered, and died for us because God loves us.

God's love was the fountain.

The birth and sufferings and death of Christ were the stream that flowed out from that fountain.

Jesus came into the world to tell us of the love of God, and to be, Himself, the proof of that love.

This is what He taught us when He uttered those wonderful words: John 3: 16—" God so loved the world etc."

Bethlehem is one of the most interesting places in Palestine. It was the home of Naomi and Ruth, and Boaz and David. And it was at Bethlehem where Jesus was born.

Praise God for this great gift.

Why did God incarnate Himself in Jesus?

First, to reveal to us His real nature, to make known to us His fatherly heart.

Jesus came speaking of His Father and our Father, and brought Him so near that we could almost see His face.

How can the joy spoken of by the angel become ours?

We cannot know the fulness of that joy, unless under the power of the Holy Spirit we take the Lord Jesus Christ to be our all in all, and make Him the Fountain of our intensest delight, and say He is my Saviour, my Christ, my Lord.

If we can say that, then the joy of which the angel spoke shall be ours.

2.—GOD'S GREAT GIFT TO THE WORLD.

2 Cor. 9: 15.—*Thanks be unto God for His unspeakable Gift.*

Paul here refers to Jesus Christ as God's great gift to the world. A gift we have all reason to be thankful for.

Peter speaks of joy unspeakable.

And Paul says he was caught up into Paradise and heard unspeakable words.

God has revealed Himself, made Himself known, through the mission of Christ.

Jesus, the Son, reveals the Father. As God, He can speak for God.

Son of God and Son of Man.

Divine enough to speak to God, and human enough to speak to man.

Jesus stands for the God-centred life, and He tells us that God is interested in us. Jesus has lit up God for us, turned light upon Him, and shown us that He is our best friend. And the gift most pleasing to Him is the gift of ourselves.

Dr. Poole, of Christ Church, London, preached on the use of disappointment. It is described as a cheering sermon. Dr. Poole referred to the great Leyland Stanford University, near San Francisco. Leyland Stanford was Governor of California, and a very wealthy man. When he and Mrs. Stanford took their only boy to Italy, he suddenly died. Only 9 years of age. The parents were broken-hearted, but they said all the children of California shall be our children," and Mr. Stanford built and endowed the magnificent University, with a gift of Twenty-two Million Dollars.

This great gift has enabled many young people to enjoy a University education.

Mr. and Mrs. Stanford were not soured. The death of their boy was the means of helping many others. This was a great gift, but God's is much greater.

Thanks be unto God for His unspeakable gift.

God has stooped to your needs and mine, by making it possible to know Him through His Son.

And when Jesus saw that His disciples did not understand Him, He said "He that hath seen Me hath seen the Father."

In coming to Jesus, we come to God. We only understand God through Jesus.

It is the will of God that all should be saved.

But salvation is a gift.

And a gift is worth nothing until it is received.

And man being free can refuse the gift.

Many receive and get the blessing; others refuse and miss the blessing.

We are all worth saving, and God is willing and anxious to save us.

He only understands Christianity who has felt it.

Christianity is not a proposition to be discussed, but a gospel to be received.

Jesus Christ came into the world to save sinners, says Paul.

That flash of light, on the Damascus road, though for a time it struck him blind, was a great eye-opener.

He understood the scriptures and the mission of Jesus much better after.

Paul learned of a love broader and deeper than anything he had thought of before.

After this, he speaks of the gospel as good news.

And a faithful saying and the pardon of sin.

What a meaning that word, salvation, had for Paul.

And what a blessing to the world, that Christ and Paul met.

Salvation—the greatest word in the Christian religion.

It means redemption from sin to the spiritual service of God.

It is not an act performed before us, but within us.

It is something that cannot be passed into the human soul like a stream of electric force.

There must be a willingness to receive it.

And when the heart is opened to the influence of the Holy Spirit, the Divine life is given to man.

Our great need is to know God, through Jesus Christ and *the Bible*.

" Bring me the book " said Sir Walter Scott, as he lay dying. " What book ? " asked his son-in-law. " The

Book," said the great book-writer, " there is only one—
the Bible."

Towards the end of the 18th century, Voltaire said in
100 years the Bible would be forgotten. 100 years have
long since passed away, and many books, which were once
popular, including some books which Voltaire himself wrote,
are gone. But the Book—the Bible—remains more con-
spicuously than ever. Millions are being sold every year.
No, no, not forgotten, and never will be.

The Bible has something to say to the world, and that is
why it lives.

Men want to know something about God, and to get
near to God, and the Bible shows the way.

It reveals to man a Saviour from sin, a Comforter in
sorrow.

For the Christ who speaks through the Book says : " *Come
unto Me*."

Nineteen centuries have given us nothing so divine as
the teaching of Jesus.

Nothing so God-like as Jesus Himself. Nothing so
satisfying as the Gospel. Nothing so revolutionising as
the Cross.

When the world wants to know God, it listens to Christ,
who says : " When ye pray, say our Father."

When it wants to see God, it looks into Christ's own face.

And so long as men are men, and sin is sin, ; so long as
the world has a conscience and a heart ; and so long as life
has temptation, and sorrow, and trial ; and so long as
the world regards the Bible as the Book, and calls for it in

the hour of need, neither Voltaire, nor thousands of Voltaires can destroy it.

The Bible is a book of religious experience. A book in which the writers have portrayed God as they know Him.

The men of the Bible are sinners, seeking after God.

Let us take courage, even from their failings, seeing we are in company with men like ourselves.

When men are anxious to live a better life, and they get to know that Christ is always ready to help them, what wonderful changes have taken place when that help has been given. Here is a case :—

A Mr. Bateson, who has been an Army Chaplain, tells of a man who said to him : " I want to give up the drink, but I cannot." " Here is a pledge card, sign it." " I have signed dozens of 'em. They are no good." Then you must have promised dozens of times to ask God to help you. You can't do it alone."

" Do you mean, pray ? " " Yes." " I don't know how to pray."

" God wants to help you, He wants to be your Friend."

" Does God want to be my Pal ? " " Yes, your Pal."

" May I ask Him now ? " " Yes." He knelt down. " O God, Mr. Bateson here says you want to be my Pal. I don't want to get drunk any more. Please help me not to ? " He rose. " I think I can do it now, sir. I feel different here," putting his hand on his breast. He became a leader among his comrades, many doing as he had done.

When C. A. Berry was a young minister in Bolton, one night he was sitting in his study with his house slippers on. It was after 12 o'clock, and he was cosy. Presently the bell rang, and he went to the door. There stood a girl with a shawl over her head and clogs on her feet. "Are you a minister?" she asked. "Yes," he answered. "You must come with me quickly, I want you to get my mother in." He thought the mother was drunk, and that she wanted someone to get her home. "You must go and get a policeman," he said. "My mother is dying, she said, " and I must bring you to get her into heaven." She lived a mile and a half away, and Berry asked could she not get another minister. "Yes, but I want you and you must come. My mother is dying." He still lingered, but she took hold of his arm, and said: "O man of God, make haste, my mother is dying." He went with her. She lived at a low public house. When he got to her bedside, he told of Jesus, the example, the Teacher. But she tossed about on her pillow. "Mister," she said, "that's no use for the likes of me. I am a sinner. I have lived my life. Cannot you tell me of somebody who can have mercy upon me and save my poor soul." He stood in the presence of the dying woman and had nothing to tell her. He jumped back to his mother's knee and cradle faith, and talked to her as his mother would have talked to her. She looked at him through her tears, and said: "Now you are getting at it; now you are helping me." He told her the story, and got her in. And, blessed be God, he got himself in. Minister as he was, he got a spiritual uplift.

Reader! Is God speaking to you?

If so, lay hold of your golden opportunity. Delay is always fraught with danger.

So much depends upon the choice you make.

Yield to the Divine pleading, and surrender your heart to Christ, and all will be well.

Lord, help us to work and live in such a way that Jesus may be able to say : well done, well done.

3.—CONVERSION AND THE KINGDOM OF GOD.

What did Jesus mean by the New Birth and Regeneration ?

In the thought of Jesus, it has something to do with the Kingdom of God.   But what did He mean by the Kingdom of God ?   It meant something He had come to establish.

The Kingdom Jesus came to establish was the kingdom of rightness, right doing.

And what He meant by being born again had reference to the kingdom.

Born of the Spirit into a kingdom of Uprightness, Holiness, Godliness, Equity, Justice, Rightfulness, Integrity, Honesty, Faithfulness.

Those who are born into this kingdom will do to others as they would like others do to them.

An Indian, hearing the golden rule explained, said " It cannot be done." Then after a pause he added : " If the

Great Spirit would give a man a new heart it might be done but not else."

The teaching of Jesus clashed with the teaching of the Jewish Teachers about the Kingdom.

The Jews thought that the Kingdom of God was National, and that they were that Nation or Kingdom.

But Jesus tried to show them that the Kingdom of Heaven was moral and spiritual.

A Kingdom of grace and glory.

At Athens, there were two Temples. A Temple of Virtue, and a Temple of Honour. And there was no going into the Temple of Honour but through the Temple of Virtue.

So the Kingdom of grace and glory are so joined together that we cannot go into the Kingdom of glory but through the Kingdom of grace.

The Kingdom of God is a state of the soul, and to give the people an idea how it worked in the life, Jesus said it was like leaven working in the dough, or like seed sown silently in the ground. The Kingdom of Heaven comes to earth just in proportion as the rebellious wills of men are replaced by the acknowledged will of God.

The Kingdom of God is not a matter of heaven only.

Man enters the Kingdom of God the moment he engages to follow Christ. God has a Kingdom on earth as well as in heaven. And the sphere of that Kingdom is the sphere of Christ's service.

Conviction and conversion.

There may be irresistible conviction, but never irresistible conversion.

Paul could not help being spoken to by Jesus, but nothing compelled him to ask " What shall I do, Lord ? "

The call of the Gospel may be regarded as two-fold—the External and the Internal.

By the external I mean the general call such as we have in the Bible, and that comes through the preaching of the Gospel.

The internal call comes when the Holy Spirit accompanies the word.

When does a man become a Christian ?   When does a seed become a plant ?   When it strikes a root down and a stem comes up.

When is a man a Christian ?   When he accepts Christ.

An intelligent young man had a talk with a Missionary, who told him what he thought was necessary to become a Christian.   " Is that it ? " said the man.   " Yes, that is it."   " Then," said he, " I am going to live that life."   In this case it was a purely intellectual decision.

Ruskin said : " He who offers God a second place, offers Him nothing."

Livingstone's Sunday School Teacher said to him : " Now, lad, make religion the every-day business of your life, and not a thing of fits and starts.   Let God have the best."

H. W. Beecher said, I had charge of a Bible Class when I was 18 years of age.

I took the subject of the relations of Christ to men out of the four Gospels, and presented it to the Class in that way, gathering everything we could about Christ.

And Beecher said : I saw Him as a personal friend, one who knows how to be sorry for the unconverted man, for the sinner.

Sorry as the Nurse, or the Mother, is sorry for the child, because it is sick

Then I said: that is God.

God's power is offered to those who are bad, to help them out of their badness.

The nature of love is to make things lovely.

The nature of purity is to make things pure.

The nature of holiness is to inspire holiness among men.

And it is the nature of God to take the poor, the needy, and the feeble in His arms, and to help them, and while He is doing this, loving them all the time.

When we get to know this God, the Christ God, who can help loving Him, and *serving Him willingly* ?

4.—A Pardoning God.

Micah 7: 18—*Who is a God like unto Thee, that pardoneth iniquity because He delighteth in mercy.*

God having promised to bring back His people out of captivity, the prophet, on that occasion, admires pardoning mercy.

As it was their sin that brought them into bondage, so it was God's pardoning their sin that brought them out of it.

The gracious God is ready to pass by and pardon the iniquity and transgression of His people, upon their repentance and return to Him.

God delights in mercy, and the salvation of sinners is what He has pleasure in.   Not their death.

O, my people, what have I done unto thee, and wherein have I wearied thee?

Testify against Me.   For I brought thee up out of the land of Egypt, and redeemed thee out of the house of servants.

He hath showed thee, O man, what is good.

And what doth the Lord require of thee but to do justly, and to love mercy, and to walk humbly with thy God.

But in every conversion there are two movements.

The movement from man to God is as needful as the movement from God to man.

Divine pity moves down to men, and human trust moves up to God.

There are two forces that now seek to rule our lives, the force that tends downwards and the force that tends upwards.

The glory of God is in forgiving sin.   There is no God like unto Him.

Has God forgiven us our transgressions?   If so we may well say, who is a God like unto Thee?

He pardoneth iniquity because He delighteth in mercy.

Dr. Alexander Whyte says: I took this text when going up and down among the people, at death-beds and sick-beds. He pardoneth iniquity, because He delighteth in mercy.

He had some Church business with a very noted lawyer. After finishing the Church business, he pushed aside pens and parchment and looked across the table at me. He said: " Have you any word for an old sinner like me ? " " He pardoneth iniquity because He delighteth in mercy," said Dr. Whyte, and slipped out. Next morning, says Dr. Whyte, I received a letter from him. " Dear friend," he said, " I was at hell's gate to-day. I was in great darkness, and no word of God could have been more helpful than the one you gave me."

He pardoneth iniquity, because He delighteth in mercy.

When I am overcome and in darkness and distress, I will always face the devil and my own conscience, and God's accusing law with that. Yes, I will say it is true. He pardoneth iniquity because He delighteth in mercy.

An old sailor once said: those words saved my soul from shipwreck, 40 years ago.

He pardoneth iniquity, because He delighteth in mercy.

Queen Victoria, a girl of 18. Lord Melbourne has arrived with a budget of papers, all of which require her attention, some her signature. Among them are some documents relating to a wretched man, who, convicted of a terrible crime, lies in a condemned cell, awaiting the hour of execution. And must I become a party to his death ? asks the young Queen. I fear that is so, replies the statesman, unless your Majesty desires to exercise your royal prerogative of mercy. The young Queen asks him to explain his meaning, and finding to her delight that she has it in her power to pardon the guilty man, she announces that, as an expression of the spirit in which she desires to rule, she proposes on this first occasion to avail herself of her authority, and she writes the word pardoned across the paper.

The young Queen was pleased when she knew that she could write the word pardoned.

Think of the God that Christ has revealed to the world.

He delighteth in mercy.

He shall cast all their sins into the depths of the sea. The depths of the sea. We seldom realise their immensity.

Mr. John Murray, an eminent authority on the subject, points out that the land is as nothing compared with the sea. The land area of the globe is only about one-third of the water area.

The mean height of the land above sea level is 2,000 feet. The mean depth of the ocean is 14,000 feet. The bulk of dry land is 23 million cubic miles. The bulk of water is 323 millions. You could hurl all your Continents and Islands into the depths of the sea, and they would all be hidden beneath two miles of water.

He pardoneth iniquity, because He delighteth in mercy.

And this pardoning God says I will cast all thy sins into the depths of the sea.

Your sins 14,000 feet into the depths of the sea.

Come, come to His feet and lay open your story of suffering and sorrow, of guilt, and of shame.

For the pardon of sin is the crown of His glory, and the joy of our Lord to be true to His name.

That thought must have helped many a doubting sinner.

The pardon of sin, the crown of His glory.

He pardoneth iniquity because He delighteth in mercy.

5.—DIVINE AND HUMAN NATURE.

Matt. 7: 11.—*If ye, then, being evil, know how to give good gifts unto your children, how much more shall your Father, which is in heaven, give good things to them that ask Him.*

The argument of Jesus is from the heart of man to the heart of God.

The way in which he proved God's goodness was to show the goodness that is to be found in the human heart.

Jesus argued upwards, from man to God, from the human to the Divine.

From what is sympathetic and loving in man to what is far more sympathetic and loving in God.

If ye know how to give good gifts, how much more your Father, which is in heaven.

As if Jesus had said, you want to know what God is.

You want to know whether He loves, and pities, and blesses ? Look into your own hearts.

Measure the tenderness, the sympathy, the care, the self-denial, the loving service, the unwearied devotion, of which you are capable.

And then look up to God and see in Him the inexhaustable fountain of all good.

All that is best in you came from Him.

Your care and love are but a dim reflection of His love and care.

You are kind ; God is infinitely kinder.

You are tender towards the suffering ; God is more tender.

You are ready to bear the burden of the afflicted ; God is more ready.

Your love will stand the long strain of years ; God's love stands the long strain of eternity.

Your limited nature can take to your heart only a few ; God, in whom there are no limitations, can take to His heart the whole human family.

The Almighty power is an all-embracing love.

That was the teaching of Jesus.

The God to whom real prayer is made must care for us as a race and as individuals.

We know God through Jesus, and He always spoke of Him as a loving Father, who loves and cares, pities and forgives.

Jesus knew God, and He never had the shadow of a doubt that God is love.

I

How much more !   A good father is kind and loving.
How *much more God !*   A good father provides for the
needs of His children.   How much more God !   A good
father gives counsel and guidance and help to his children.
How much more God !

Take everything that the best father can do, every pro-
vision he can make, every care he can bestow.   Take all
the love and sympathy he can give, and multiply it thousands of times, if you would know the value of that how
much more.

When we come to know in some measure the value of
those words, we shall trust God with everything.

With our present and with our future we are the Father's
chief concern.   What a help it would be if we could believe
it.   Then we should be able to say :

> Were the whole realm of Nature mine,
> That were a present far too small ;
> Love, so amazing, so divine,
> Demands my soul, my life, my all.

That is to say, my soul is a greater and bigger thing
than the whole realm of nature.

God's care for His children.

A King is sitting with his council, deliberating on high
affairs of state, involving the destiny of nations, when
suddenly he hears the sorrowful cry of his little child, who
has fallen down or been frightened by a wasp.   He rises
and runs to his relief, assuages his sorrow and relieves his
fears.

How much more your Heavenly Father, whose ear is quicker than any human ear, will run to your relief!

This is the true method of teaching: climbing up, step by step, from the human to the divine.

6.—THE GOLDEN RULE.

The Golden Rule—*Doing to others as you would like others to do to you.*

Phil. 2: 3-4.—*Let nothing be done through strife or vain glory; but in lowliness of mind let each esteem others better than themselves.*

> *Look not every man on his own things, but every man also on the things of others. Therefore all things whatsoever ye would that men should do to you, do ye even so to them.*

Luke 10, 25, 26, 27 and 28.—*And behold a certain lawyer stood up and tempted Him, tested Him, saying: " Master what shall I do to inherit eternal life ? "*

> *And Jesus said unto him: " What is written in the law, how readest thou ? "*

> *And he, answering said: " Thou shalt love the Lord thy God with all thy heart, and with all thy soul, and with all thy strength, and with all thy mind, and thy neighbour as thyself."*

> *And Jesus said unto him: " Thou hast answered right ; this do, and thou shalt live."*

There is a good story told of Turner, the artist.

A young man had sent a picture to the academy, and Turner said to the Committee : " We must find a good place for this young man's picture."

" Impossible," said the others, " No room." He did not argue with them.

He took down one of his own and put the young man's in its place.

On another occasion when his picture of Cologne was hung between two portraits, the painter of the portraits said that Turner's bright sky had thrown his pictures into the shade..

At the private view, a friend of Turner's, who had seen the Cologne in all its splendour, led some friends to see the picture. The man started back in amazement. The golden sky had become dim, and the glory was gone. He ran up to the artist, Turner. " Turner, what have you been doing ? " " Oh, " whispered Turner, " poor Lawrence was so unhappy. Its only damp-black. It will all wash off after exhibition."

A beautiful comment upon the golden rule.

Making others happy. We shall never lessen the light of our own candle by lighting another.

" I mean to have a good time," said a girl, a short time ago. She meant that she was going to neglect everything but her own pleasure, and was going to trouble about nobody but herself.

But she will find that a really good time cannot come that way.

Our Master has so linked us up with one another that we really belong to each, and all to Him, and those who are really the happiest, and have the best time, are always those who seek another's good.

Dr. Jowett, speaking about the influence of kind words and kind actions, says :

We release the best in ourselves when we release the best in others.

It is a law in life that when we busy ourselves in liberating the best in others our own best begins to emerge.

We ourselves are more fully emancipated as we seek another's freedom.

We ourselves are warmed at the fire which we kindled for another.

It has been said that if we bring happiness into the lives of others we shall not be able to keep it out of our own.

The bee that serves the flowers by its visits brings wealth to its own hive.

Religion is the Divine side of philanthropy.   Philanthropy is the practical side of religion.

Tom Paine once said to a noted minister : " What a pity it is that a man has not some comprehensive and perfect rule for the government of his life."

The minister replied : " There is such a rule, viz :— " Love to God and love to thy neighbour."

" Oh," said Paine, " That is in your Bible," and walked away.

George Washington's idea of life was to pluck up thistles and plant flowers.

If we live only for pleasure, there will soon be little pleasure in living.

If you want to become great, render service.

" This do," said Jesus, " and thou shalt live."

What had the lawyer to do ?   To love the Lord, his God, with all his heart, and with all his soul, and with all his strength, and with all his mind.

Love is life.   Only he who loves lives.

Only love can get out of a man the deepest secrets of his being.

The law goes still further than love to God.   It includes one's neighbour.   Love thy neighbour as thyself.

Love of God means love of man.

We must first of all be right with God, or we never can be right with man.   God first, man after.

Ahab would not have done the deed of Jezreel if his soul had contained the slightest love for Naboth.

Love begets love.   God's love is the point from which to move the soul.   We cannot love because we must.   Must kills love.

To love God with the heart is to delight in pleasing Him. And to look upon ourselves and all we have as belonging to Him.

Thou shalt love thy neighbour as thyself..

Can it be done ?

But who is my neighbour ?   Every man in distress.

The Samaritan had compassion on the wounded man— compassion—a sensation of sorrow, excited by the distress or misfortunes of another.

He drew out his sympathetic soul, first of all, and wrapped that warmly around him, and made him understand that smaller gifts and minor mercies would soon be forthcoming.

The oil, the wine, the bandages, the beast, the inn, the pence, the care, are all only so many forms of the large-hearted compassion with which the good Samaritan started.

You see the same when Jesus had compassion upon the multitude.   After the compassion came the feeding of the people.

Sympathy is two hearts tugging at one load and bent beneath one sorrow.

The first step God took towards making us become like Him was for Him to become like us.

The parable of the Good Samaritan must have helped thousands of people.   What is it that gives strength to this parable ?

This : that it tells men they are to help their fellow-men. Not because that they are of the same race, the same religion, the same sect or party, but because they are men.   This parable of the Good Samaritan commands us to be humane, to exercise humanity, which signifies kindness to all human beings, simply because they are human beings.

The more men you know and love, the richer souls you are.

And the joy of joys, and the grandest of joys, that is doing something to help other people.

A man is rich or poor according to what he is, not according to what he has.

The great principle of life is the principle of the golden rule.　We are to put ourselves in the place of others, and then think what we would like done to us.

7.—THE TWO PATHS.

Jer. 21: 8.—*And unto this people thou shalt say: Thus saith the Lord; Behold I set before you the way of life, and the way of death.*

Rom. 6: 23.—*For the wages of sin is death; but the gift of God is eternal life through Jesus Christ our Lord.*

Joshua, 24: 15.—*Choose you this day whom ye will serve.*

Think of the Bible as a guide book, pointing out the path of safety and the path of danger.　The path of life and the path of death.

We all need direction in our life.　In all thy ways acknowledge Him and He shall direct thy paths.

The hard ways as well as the easy ways, the thorny paths as well as the paths of flowers.

One of the boys of Christiana, when having a little talk with Greatheart about the pilgrimage, said: " I remember now what my mother said: " The way to heaven is as up a ladder, and the way to hell is as down a hill.　But I would rather go up a ladder to life than down the hill to death."

Youth is one of the precious opportunities of life.　Rich in blessings, if you choose to make it so.

But having in it the materials of undying remorse if you suffer it to pass unimproved.

You may rebel at responsibility, but you cannot escape it

If you go wrong, you fight against God.   If you go right, you are co-workers with God.

If you fail, and fall, and spoil your life, it will to some extent be your fault.

If I bring before you the good and the bad, it is that I may help you to choose the good.

I want to find you before you are lost.

You can do more by being good than in any other way.

Christianity has nothing to fear.   It turns out the grandest men in the world.

I want to impress you with this thought, that God is seeking you.

We do not need to search for Him.   He is the Shepherd, we the sheep.   We need to let Him find us.

God is after us.

The God-life in my life is seeking for me.

I am come that they might have life.   I am still here to give you life.

Some years ago, two young men left home to attend college.   Whilst at college, revival services were being held in a Church near by.   One said to the other : " Shall we go ? "   " I don't want to, but I will walk down the street with you."

He pleaded with him to go in, but he would not.

At the end of their course at college the two men separated.

Years after, the one who went into the Church and gave himself to God and had become a preacher of the Gospel was going to preach in the same Church where he was converted.

He is spoken to by a tramp, who proved to be the man who refused to go into the Church.

And the miserable outcast said : " Do you recall the day you pleaded so earnestly with me to go with you into yon Church ? From that very hour I date my misery and downfall. God called, but *I answered not.*"

The life of the soul is *Union with God.*

The death of the soul is *Separation from God.*

Paul seems to say every man has two masters, either of whom he may serve.

He may be the servant of sin. Then he must take its wages, which are slavery and death.

He may be the servant of righteousness. Then he will have all the freedom and energy life is capable of.

The whole Gospel is summed up in this contrast—What we are by nature, and what we are by grace.

God divides the world into two classes, under different figures—good, bad, righteous, wicked, sheep, goats, wheat, chaff.

Paul delights in contrasts, and he says : " The works of the flesh are manifest, which are these : adultery, fornication, uncleanliness, lasciviousness, idolatry, witchcraft, hatred, variance, emulations, wrath, strife, seditions, heresies, envyings, murders, drunkenness, revellings, and such like ; of the which I tell you before, as I have told you in time past, that they which do such things shall not inherit the Kingdom of God.   But the fruit of the Spirit is love, joy, peace, long-suffering, gentleness, goodness, faith, meekness, temperance ; against such there is no law."

Sin : What it is and what it does.

To our lower nature sin is pleasant ; to our higher nature, sin is bondage and degradation.

Man has two sides to his being.   The one akin to nature, the other akin to God.

The New Birth is the gift of God to man.

On the Divine side it is a gift.   On the human side, it is receiving the gift.

Sin :   What does it mean ?

It means missing the mark to keep on telling people they must not do this, that, or the other.

Is not the best way to make them feel drawn to religion ?

Anything that stops the best from developing in me is wrong, because it makes me miss the mark that my life was meant to reach.

Anything that stops my better self from flourishing is sin.

Religion has no quarrel with brightness or happiness, or any thing else, so long as it helps us to hit the mark.   That is, the right mark.

Anything and everything that helps to develop the best that is in me, that is of God.

Anything and everything that prevents, that is sin.

Side by side with this is another and very practical test of right and wrong.   The effect on other people.

As we go through life, we come into touch with all kinds of men and women, and we never leave them as we find them.

What we say or do either helps to drag them down or lift them up.

If I conquer a temptation, I lift humanity nearer to God. When I play fast and loose with life and duty, I drag others deeper into the mire.

If this is so, and I believe it is, it is nonsense to say that every man has a right to live his own life in his own way.

No man liveth to himself.

Any pleasure that has to be paid for by the physical or moral injury of others, any whim or bad temper that spoils the life of a home, anything that betrays the trust imposed in us, stands condemned without a moment's argument.

There is an influence and a power in a good life.   There is an influence and a power in a bad life.   Good thinking is life, bad thinking is death.

A man once said, while arguing with another, " I am not convinced by what you say.   But one thing I cannot understand; it puzzles me, and makes me feel a power in what you say.   It is, why you should care enough for me to take all this trouble and labour with me as if you cared for my soul."

Thou must be true thyself,
  If thou the truth wouldst teach ;
Thy soul must overflow, if thou
  Another's soul would reach ;
It needs the overflow of heart
  To give the lips full speech.

The greatest uplift in life is the allowing of the larger man to overcome the meaner.

Man must serve, his only choice being which of two masters he will serve. Satan or God, sin or righteousness, He cannot serve both.

Choose you this day whom ye will serve.

The Christian life is not something to be set up and admired from afar. It is something to be lived out every day.

We can help God by letting Him help us.

To as many as received Him, to them gave He power to become the sons of God.

The Spirit of life in Christ Jesus frees men from the law of sin and death.

Jesus Christ does that for men which no other being has been able to do.

He raises men from the death of sin to the life of righteousness. He kindles within them love, and pity, and self sacrifice. He gives them new hopes, new aims, new life from God.

Don't worry too much about the things you are in doubt about, but hang on with all your weight to the things about which you are certain and bind them to your heart.

Let God have your best.

Then He will be able to give you His best.

What is God's best ?

The gift of Himself. And He is more willing to give Himself than parents are to give bread to their children.

When we think of all the promises that the Christian can claim, and all the joy that comes into his life by serving God, and helping others to Christ, the Saviour of men, we ought never to speak of such a life as a sacrifice. Is it a sacrifice to drop tinsel and pick up gold, or sin's pleasure to get the deep joy of the Lord ?

8.—DANIEL'S VISION.

Dan. 10: 7.—*And I, Daniel, alone saw the vision ; for the men that were with me saw not the vision ; but a great quaking fell upon them, so that they fled to hide themselves.*

Vision : the art of seeing.

But in scripture language it implies a supernatural appearance, by which God made His will known.

From the earliest times He appeared to patriarchs and prophets and holy men in vision.

Sometimes by dreams during the night, and sometimes by angels during the day.

Whereby their minds were illuminated.

Daniel was a prophet, raised up by God during the captivity of the Jews in Chaldea.

At an early age he was carried prisoner to Babylon, B.C. 606.

At the Court of Babylon he was soon raised to offices of trust and honour, and became first Minister to the King.

He survived the captivity, but being very far advanced in life it is supposed that he never returned to his native land, but died in Shu-Shan, in the third year of Cyrus, B.C. 534.

Josephus says Daniel showed Cyrus the prophecies of Isaiah which related to him.

Is. 44, 28.—That saith of Cyrus, *He is* my Shepherd, and shall perform all my pleasure : even saying to Jerusalem, Thou shalt be built ; and to the temple, Thy foundation shall be laid.

He gave every facility to the Jewish exiles to return to their own land, and restored to them the sacred vessels which Nebuchadnezzar had carried away.   He also arranged for the expense of re-building the Temple to be defrayed from the Royal treasury.

In the third year of Cyrus, King of Persia, a thing was revealed unto Daniel, and the thing was true, but the time appointed was long.   And he understood the thing, and had understanding of the vision.

He goes on to say : " I was by the side of the great river Hid-de-kel, or Tigris.   Then I lifted up mine eyes and looked, and behold a certain man clothed in linen, whose loins were girded with fine gold."

Daniel was mourning for his own sins and the sins of his people.

Many of the Jews who had liberty to return to their own land continued in the land of captivity, not knowing how to value the privileges offered them.

Daniel's place was Babylon, but their place was Jerusalem, helping to build the temple.

Or he might be troubled when he heard of the opposition the Jews were receiving from their enemies.

Good men cannot but mourn to see how slow the work of God goes on in the world, and what opposition it meets with.

It was during this time that Daniel had the vision, and the person he saw could be no other than Christ Himself.

He was by the side of the great river Tigris, and being a person of distinction, he had his servants attending him at some distance.

There he looked up and saw one man, one alone, a certain man, even the man Christ Jesus. It must be He, for He appears in the same resemblance wherein He appeared to John, in the Isle of Patmos.

His dress was priestly, for He is the High Priest of our profession. Clothed in linen.

His loins were girded with a golden girdle of finest gold. Not only a Priest, but a King.

" Now let my Lord speak," says Daniel, " for I can hear it, and I can bear it, and am ready to do according to it, for Thou hast strengthened me."

Lord, give what Thou commandest, and then command what Thou wilt.

Daniel gets the assurance that his prayers were come up for a memorial before God.

Fear not, Daniel, I am with thee.

Isaiah had a vision, for he says : " Mine eyes hath seen the Lord."

Uz-ziah came to the throne when a lad of 16. For more than 50 years he reigned in Jerusalem, wisely and well.

And it was when this good king died that Isaiah had the vision.

Life is full of change. Isaiah was a young man, picturing a dark future. But with the vision he got to know something of the Eternal King. And when He reigns things will be better.

The Prophet had lost a hero when the King died, but he found His Lord.

He anticipated chaos, and lo, in place of chaos, there emerged the Lord of Order.

We have feared the withering blast of death. What will Isaiah do when Uz-ziah is taken ?

Isaiah anticipated an end, but he found a beginning.

In a very deep and true sense it is what a man sees that either makes or unmakes him.

The effect of vision upon character and service is transforming. It elevates or debases, according to its quality.

K

For seven years Dr. Thomas Chalmers occupied a pulpit and preached with splendid eloquence before he had an experience in his own soul of the renewing power of God.

He has left on record the sad and humiliating testimony that his preaching during those years did not have the weight of a feather on the morals of his parishioners.

But the day came when he was laid aside by illness. In this illness he saw the King—the Lord of Hosts. In that vision he saw himself, and his heart was broken with contrition. The formal gave way to the vital, and the professional to the real.

And the whole man was transformed. His health returned, he went back to his pulpit, and all Scotland was shaken.

9.—GOD'S LOVE FOR THE YOUNG.

Prov. 8 : 17 and 36.—*I love them that love Me, and those that seek me early shall find Me.*

But he that sinneth against me wrongeth his own soul.

They that love the Lord Jesus Christ in sincerity shall be loved of Him, and those who seek Him in a right way shall find Him.

Jesus used words almost identical with these, for He said : " If any man love Me, I will manifest Myself to him ; I will make Myself known to him," etc.

Wonderful things in the Bible I see,
This is the dearest, that Jesus loves me.

Take those three last words : Jesus loves me, and repeat them five or six times, then think about it.   Jesus loves me.

If everybody could believe that, we should have a new world.

Jesus loves me.   May God help us to see it.

And believe it.

We should know more of Christ if we loved Him more.

Those who seek Me early shall find Me.   This is very encouraging to young folks.   Christ is near you, and He wants you to know it.   He cannot force Himself upon you.

But He would be delighted if you would stretch out your hand, and open your heart, and say : Blessed Jesus, take charge of my life and tell me what I ought to do.

We know now that Christ is everywhere, in all power, in all light, in all wisdom, in all truth, in all love.

He found Himself in Moses, in the Prophets, in the Psalms, and in all the Scriptures.

The Apostles have not hesitated to declare that he was before all things, and that by Him all things were created, and without Him was not anything made that was made.

In the beginning was the word, etc.

I have never seen as much in Christ as I see to-day.

> I lift my heart to Thee, Saviour divine ;
> For Thou art all to me, and I am Thine.
> Is there on earth a closer bond than this :
> That my Beloved's mine, and I am His.

You cannot destroy the message of Jesus. Men will always want it.

He answers the riddles of the human heart.

Humanity seems to be groping after God. And Jesus says : " Take my hand, and I will lead you to God."

Human wisdom cannot discover God.

Paul went to Athens—at that time perhaps the greatest city in the world. But what did he find there ? An Altar with the inscription : To the Unknown God.

All the wisdom of Greece had not found God.

Jesus is the safe and supreme Teacher. You may trust Him.

Gladstone said, a few years before he passed away : " The longer I live, the more I am persuaded that the old, old story of Jesus and His love is the one hope of humanity."

Jesus Christ was the visible image of the Invisible God.

The manifestation of the Unseen Father. He and the Father were one. And all that He was and did, the Father was and did through Him.

His heart was the Father's heart, His thoughts the Father's thoughts, His purposes the Father's purposes, and His sacrifice the Father's sacrifice.

He that sinneth against Me wrongeth his own soul.

What can appear worse than hating Him who is the centre of all beauty, the fountain of all goodness, love itself.

They that offend Christ do the greatest wrong to themselves. They wrong their own souls, they wound their own consciences.

They deceive themselves, disturb themselves, destroy themselves.

The word sin, as we have it in the text, means missing the mark.

He that misseth Me, he that sinneth against Me, wrongeth his own soul.

He who neglects, hazards his life as truly as he who ventures to transgress the physical laws of his being.

Indeed, neglect may be a real transgression of the most vital things of life.

Sin, when it hath conceived, bringeth forth death.

Sin, therefore, is moral insanity, with a dagger in its hand. The end of it is self-murder.

Misseth Me. Who is this who is speaking wisdom ?

But we have no difficulty in speaking of wisdom and Christ as one and the same.

For the Psalmist takes up the same note, and cries : " The fear of the Lord is the beginning of wisdom. And the knowledge of the Holy is understanding."

It is therefore God whom the sinner misses.

The world has missed God because it has looked for Him in the wrong way, and in the wrong direction.

It has looked for Him without.

It should first have looked for Him within. For He dwells in contrite hearts.

And the Kingdom of God is within you.

And the soul is restless till it finds rest in God.

No true life is possible without God.

When Jesus came into the life of Paul, he was able to say to King Agrippa : " I was not disobedient to the heavenly vision."

It was there and then that Paul's life really began. When Christ met with him.

And death begins in the case of any man when he shuts his eyes to the call of God, and is disobedient to the vision which God gives him.

If the statement of the Apostle—In Him we live—is true, then the proposition must also be true that out of Him, or without Him, we die.

The life of the soul is union with God ; the death of the soul is separation from God.

Jesus did not hesitate to say :

I am the way—Without Me there is no going.

I am the truth—Without me there is no knowing.

I am the Light—Without Me there is no seeing.

I am the Life—Without Me there is no living.

The earth has no sadder sight than that of an immortal soul denying the Bread of Life, and starving to death on husks.

There is something worse than a starved body, and that is a starved soul.

Jesus was always telling His disciples that a great soul was far better than a full barn.

May the Lord make us wise unto salvation.

To do wrong is an injury to God, and an injury to the man guilty of that wrong himself.

Jesus wants us to have something which will help us to live the good and useful life.

Here it is—In the way of righteousness is life, and in the pathway thereof there is no death.

10.—THE PROMISE TO THOSE WHO WAIT ON GOD.

Isa. 40 : 31.—*They that wait upon the Lord shall renew their strength.*

Isa. 49 : 23.—*They shall not be ashamed that wait for Me.*

This is a word which will always be in season to them that are weary.

To wait upon the Lord, to have faith in God, to trust in the Lord.

Saving faith—The act of joining our weakness to Christ's strength, our ignorance to His knowledge, our guiltiness to His atoning love, our wills to His will, ourselves to Him.

In the year 1861, the Southern States of America were filled with slaves and slave-holders.

Abraham Lincoln became President, and he resolved to do all he could to wipe away this awful scourge from the pages of his nation's history.

Before he became the President of America, he was a lawyer, and he with other friends were riding across the prairie and through the woods. The birds sang, the sun shone, the scene and the sounds were pleasant. And as they passed through a wood they noticed a little bird had fallen from its nest. They all passed, but Lincoln turned back and helped it back to its nest. His friends waited for him. They saw him go to the spot and help the bird back to the nest. When he got back, one of them said : " Well, Lincoln, why did you trouble to go back for such a small thing as that ? " " I can only say this, I feel the better for it."

That is the right spirit.

Any one with this spirit will get the best out of life.

Abraham Lincoln had no question as to his duty to the slaves of the United States. His mind was made up that slavery must be destroyed. He once said : " If ever I get a chance to hit that evil I will hit it hard."

The chance came to him, and he struck so hard, and so repeatedly, that he lost his life in the contest, but he inflicted a blow from which slavery has not recovered and never will.

A rebellion broke out, and when Lincoln addressed the Senate the house was packed with people. Before him was gathered the business skill and the intellectual power of the States.

With one son lying dead in the White House, whom he loved with a father's affection, another little boy on the borders of eternity, with his nation's eternal disgrace, or everlasting honour, resting upon his speech, he speaks distinctly, forcefully, and without fear, Friend and foe marvel at his collected movements.   They know of the momentous issues which hang on his address.   They know the domestic trials that oppress his heart.

But they do not know that before leaving home that morning the President had taken down the Family Bible and conducted their home worship as usual, and then had asked to be left alone.   The family withdrawing, they heard his tremulous voice raised in pleadings with God.   That He, whose shoulders sustain the government of Worlds, would guide him and overrule his speech for His Own Glory.

Here was the secret of Lincoln's strength.   He knew how to wait on God.

I want to give you an idea what kind of a man he was. As a young man, Abraham Lincoln never forgot the religion he learned at his mother's knee, though she died when he was only nine years old.

He was an upright, sincere man, and a total abstainer to the day of his death.

He once said to the person who induced him to sign the pledge : " I owe more to you than to almost anyone else of whom I can think.   If I had not signed the pledge with you in my years of youthful temptation, I might have gone the way that the majority of my old comrades have gone, a drunkard's life, and a drunkard's grave.   I promised my mother only a few days before she died that I would never use anything intoxicating as a beverage, and I consider that promise as binding to-day as it was the day I gave it."

John Kitto, when a boy, put a mark against the passage : They shall not be ashamed that wait on me.

Thirty years after he says : " I believed it then, I know it now."

They shall not be ashamed that wait on Me.

They that wait upon the Lord shall renew their strength.

We are to wait upon the Lord to receive power.

A Scotch Highlander was in the habit of going every morning a little distance from his cottage, and he would stand for a few minutes.

He said to a friend : " I have come here for years, and taken off my hat to the beauty of the world."

Those who don't wait upon God miss the best.

Emerson writes : " The Creator keeps His word with us. All I have seen teaches me to trust Him for all I have not seen."

God's goodness shines forth in the face of Jesus.

When you have seen that face, you will know that God is good.

This word, wait, was used by Christ after the resurrection, and just before the ascension.

And being assembled with them on the Mount of Olives, He commanded them that they should not depart from Jerusalem, but wait for the promise of the Father, which, saith He, ye have heard of Me.

And for ten days they waited. Pentecost was a great spiritual uplift.

And Jesus, so far as His bodily presence went, was taken from them.

We now pass from the visible ministry of Christ to the invisible ministry of the Holy Ghost.   Jesus spake His last word to the Apostles, and a cloud received Him out of their sight.

Nothing more, only out of sight.

Not out of hearing.

Not out of sympathy.

Only out of sight—but we are not out of His sight.

We want sometimes to see Him, but He says : " Because ye have seen me, ye have believed."   Blessed are they which have not seen and yet have believed.   We shall one day see Him as He is.   He is out of sight, but not out of memory.

" Whom do men say I am ? "   " Thou art a Divine Being, manifest in the flesh.   Blessed art Thou," was, in effect, Simon Barjona's answer.

It is not Peter's person, but Peter's faith, that is the fundamental matter in Christ's mind.

Christ now speaks of the Church that is to be, for the first time, in connection with Simon's confession.

If the Church is built upon that confession—Thou art the Christ, the Son of the Living God, and abides on that foundation, it will stand.

Peter's confession contains the Doctrine of Christ's Divinity, and Jesus was pleased with it.

When Jesus spoke of Peter as a rock, He was indicating

that his nature should be transformed from weakness to strength.

The power of the Holy Ghost.—By that power you shall be animated and actuated by a better spirit than your own.

Peter's great change.—Before the Crucifixion, weak; after Pentecost, strong.

We wait on Christ for some brighter manifestation of His presence.

We take at His hands the soul's bread.

The condition of waiting upon the Lord must be fulfilled, before we can expect the renewal of our strength.

Religion is our deepest need, and God is our highest good.

Religion is that blessed experience in which man comes home to God.

It is fellowship with the unseen.

11.—CHRIST THE REVEALER.

The Revelation of the Father, by Jesus Christ.

No man hath seen God at any time; the only begotten Son, He hath declared Him. He visibly embodied the Father.

He made the Father intelligible. He made the Father accessible.

We are not to insist on a literal visibleness, for this is impossible, but on a manifestation so unique and distinct, as to justify the declaration : " He that hath seen Me, hath seen the Father."

He that hath seen me healing the sick and feeding the hungry, hath seen the Father doing these things.

He that hath seen me teaching the ignorant, and offering the weary rest, hath seen the Father doing these very things.

It is the invisible revealed to your eyes.

He that hath seen me seeking and saving the lost, receiving sinners and forgiving sins, hath seen the Father so doing.

He that hath seen Me, hath seen the Father.

Offering sympathy, yet escaping defilement.   Man could pity the leper, but Christ could touch Him.

How, then, is it true that they who have seen Christ hath seen the Father ?

And yet, only they have seen the Father to Whom Christ has revealed Him.

This reminds us that there is seeing and seeing.   There is a seeing which sees nothing.

Eyes have they, but they see not ; ears have they, but they hear not ; and hearts have they, but they do not understand.

To see the form of Christ is not to see the Image of the Invisible God.

To whom, then, will the Son reveal the Father ?

To the man who is humble and of a contrite heart.

The ever-living Christ.

What the Church has to believe is that Christ cannot die.

What we want strengthening in is the fundamental position that Jesus Christ must reign till He hath put all enemies under His feet.

The Christian has but one engagement, and that is to serve Christ.

There are men who can say humbly and truly : For me to live is Christ.

You can explain the Saviour's self-sacrifice and care for us in one way, and in one way only.

He gave His life for us because He loved us.

Many a man has been arrested when that thought has gripped him.   Jesus loves me.

C. H. Spurgeon tells of a man who stepped into one of the services at Exeter Hall, and was brought to Christ by the singing of the Hymn, Jesu, Lover of my soul.   "Does Christ love me ?" he said ; "then why should I live in enmity to Him ? "

If people would think a little more on these lines, there would be better results.

12.—THE WAY OF SALVATION.

Acts 16 : 30.—*What must I do to be saved ?*

This question was put by the Phililpian jailor.

The Rich young Ruler : What shall I do that I may have eternal life ?

What is salvation ?   Deliverance from sin ; not only that, it is growth in all trueness and goodness of life.   Salvation is character.

Old passions have been killed.   New affections have been born.   A new light has entered into the life and transformed it wonderfully.   The old man has been put off. The new man has been put on.

When this change has taken place, it means a life lived, not for self, but for God and mankind.

To be self-centred is to be spiritually dead, not alive.

How do I get spiritual life ?

1st—Believe, learn, accept God's gift.

Before we can give, we must drink in the very life and Spirit of God, as revealed by Jesus Christ.

Believing is relying upon or trusting.   To give ourselves up to Him.   Love in the soul, washing sin from the soul.

If we are to master the world, and master self, we must have dealings with the unseen.   That is, we must have a firm grip upon the things that are unseen.   Upon God, His grace, upon Christ and His strength.

What shall I do that I may have eternal life ?

Repentance and forgiveness.

Think of a man who has no desire for the good, and remember that one condition of forgiveness is repentance.

It is so in human relationships.   You do not forgive the

The measure of human desire is the limit of God's power to bestow.

God can only give us the best things when we hunger for them. He can only give us Himself when we are willing to receive Him.

Need and desire are the measure of our capacity to receive in every aspect of life.

The man who is contented with what he is will never grow.

Behind all progress is hunger.

How many empty hearts are empty because they did not ask and seek.

The Kingdom of God is held back because men do not want purity and honesty and comradeship and peace intensely enough.

It is only hunger which will bring them. But once get that hunger in the hearts of men everywhere, and they will come. Once the hunger is aroused, men will seek and pray and strive. The new days will come with their unimagined blessings.

It is a law which covers the whole of life that the things for which men hunger will be given, and the things for which they do not hunger must be withheld.

To every man there openeth a way, and ways, and a way.
And the high soul climbs the high way and the low soul
  gropes the low.
And in between, on the misty flats, the rest drift to and fro.
But to every man there openeth a high and a low,
And every man decideth the way his soul shall go.

The real need of the Church and the world to-day is to come into touch with the Living Christ.

A power that touches us and can be touched,

And of which we can have real and experimental knowledge.

It is life, more life, and fuller, that we want.

A very little study of history will convince us that Christianity is a great revolutionary force, if it is anything.

When once the law of Jesus Christ is applied to human life, the revolution will be at hand.

Don't talk about Christianity being played out.

Christianity, or the teaching of Christ, has never been tried.

It is necessary in these days to lay some stress upon the fact that Jesus Christ is a living force, and available for human needs.

Dr. Dale was preparing an Easter sermon, when there suddenly flashed across his mind the conviction that Jesus Christ was alive. This conviction changed the character of his preaching from that time onwards. He got a spiritual uplift.

14.—THE ALL-COMPREHENSIVE LOVE OF GOD.

John 3: 16.—*God so loved the world that He gave His only begotten Son, that whosoever believeth in Him should not perish, but have everlasting life.*

Our foreign missionaries have found John 3: 16, most effective.

" This is life eternal," said Jesus, " that they might know Thee the only true God, and Jesus Christ whom Thou hast sent."

All are yours.

Life is yours, with its joys and sorrows, lights and shades, laughter and tears, success and failures, triumphs and defeats.

Yours, as the stones and mortar and building materials are the builder's, out of which he is to construct a building.

Death is yours. Death is not only God's servant, but man's servant.

Lyman Abbott has spoken of death in a very pleasing way. He speaks of this world as God's house, in which there are many rooms. Death is only pushing aside the curtain, and passing from one room to another.

And if we think of all that Jesus said the night before the crucifixion about death and the Father's house, we must look upon Christ as the Light-bringer.

He says : " Lo, I am with you alway, even unto the end of the world." He also says : " It is expedient for you that I go away."

And yet, by going away, He comes nearer to us.

Paul's definition of dying is to depart and to be with Christ, which is far better.

For me to live is Christ, and to die is gain.

Paradise is not a distant country ; it is only the other room.

Jesus seems to say : You think I am going away, to be

as though I were not.   Not at all.   I go back to my Father, and yet, in going back to my Father, I do not go away from you.

I live ;   my Father liveth with Me ;   I live with Him, I live with you ;   I will come again and make my abode with you.

My life does not break off, does not carry me away from you ;   I continue to be in your presence and companionship more than ever before.

It is for your advantage that I go, because I can serve you better, live more with you, be closer to you, than I ever was in the flesh.

Here we have the Divine Man testifying to the truth within his own knowledge respecting the Father and the higher life.

The Light Bringer and the Deliverer.

Death has had no power over Him.   He is still with His Church to the end of time conquering and to conquer.

While we are on the earth we need the earthly body. When we pass from the earth into heaven, we shall need the heavenly body.   We cannot carry further the body we had here.   If it were raised from the grave, it would be useless, for flesh and blood cannot inherit the kingdom of God.

I want to speak a word of comfort to those who have stood looking into the open grave.

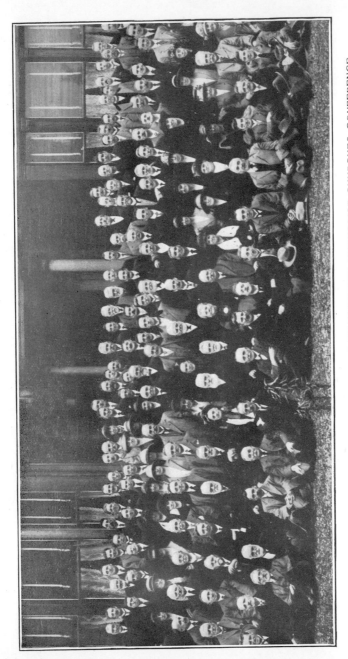

DELEGATES AND FRIENDS WHO ATTENDED THE INDEPENDENT METHODIST CHURCHES CONFERENCE, AT BETHEL CHURCH, COLNE, JUNE 16-19, 1923.

A CHAPTER OF STORIES.

When the great Evangelists, D. L. Moody and Ira D. Sankey, first came to England, in 1873, I had the pleasure of attending some of their meetings, and feeling the power of their appeal. Moody was a great teller of effective stories, and I venture to reprint two of them, together with others which I have frequently used in addresses and sermons.

THE POWER OF LOVE.

A gentleman one day came to my office for the purpose of getting me interested in a young man who had just got out of the penitentiary. "He says," said the gentleman, "he does not want to go to the office, but I want your permission to bring him in and introduce him." I said, "bring him in." The gentleman brought him and introduced him, and I took him by the hand and told him I was glad to see him. I invited him up to my house, and when I took him into my family I introduced him as a friend. When my little daughter came into the room I said, "Emma, this is papa's friend." And she went up and kissed him, and the man sobbed aloud. After the child left the room, I said, "What is the matter?" "O sir," he said, "I have not had a kiss for years. The last kiss I had was from my mother, and she was dying. I thought I would never love another one again." His heart was broken.

Just that little kindness showed I was in sympathy with him. Another young man, just out of the penitentiary, came to me, and after I had talked with him for some time, he didn't seem to think I was in sympathy with him. I offered him a little money, " No," he said, " I don't want your money." " What do you want ? " " I want some one to have confidence in me." I got down and prayed with him, and in my prayer I called him a brother, and he shed tears the moment I called him a brother. So if we are going to reach men we must make them believe we are their brothers.

LOVE CAN CONQUER.

A Sunday School Superintendent I knew had a boy in his school that nearly broke it up. He put him under one teacher and nothing could be done with him ; he put him under another teacher, and nothing could be done with him ; and he made up his mind to expel him from the school, and do it publicly, and let all the school know that the boy was expelled. But there came a lady teacher to him who said : " I wish you would let me have that boy." " But' said he, " he is such a bad boy ; he uses such vulgar language. All those men can't do anything with him, and I think I am sure you can't." The lady said, " I am not doing much for Christ, but it may be that I can win him." But she was a lady of refined society, and he thought,

" Surely, she won't be willing to have patience with that boy."

He gave her the boy, and, he said, for a few Sundays he behaved very well, but one Sunday he behaved badly, and she corrected him, and he up and spat in her face. She quietly took her handkerchief and wiped her face. I don't know what his name was, but we will call him Johnny. " Johnny," she says, " I wish you would go home with me. I want to talk with you." " Well, I won't," he said, " I won't be seen on the street with you." And what's more, I ain't never coming to this Sunday School any more." " Well," she says, " If you won't walk home with me, let me walk home with you."

No, he said he wouldn't be seen on the street with her, and he was not coming to that dirty old Sunday School any more. She knew if she was going to reach that boy she must do it then, and she thought she would try. She thought that she would just bear on that curiosity chord. Sometimes when you can't reach people in any other way, you do it by exciting their curiosity. She said to him : " If you will come to my house next Tuesday morning I shan't be there, but if you will go there and ring the front door bell, and tell the servant there is a little bundle on the bureau for you, she will give it to you." The little fellow said he wouldn't come. She thought he might change his mind. He thought it over, and he thought he would just like to know what there was in that bundle.

And he went up to the house Tuesday morning, and the bundle was handed to him ; and there was a little vest in it and a little necktie that she had made with her own hands, hearted brother, who pointed me to the great Physician who had power to cure me and heal me of my appetite, if I would only receive Him. Broken, weak, vile and helpless, I came to Him, and by His grace I was able to accept Him as my Redeemer, and I have come here to say He can save to the uttermost.

Mr. Moody interested himself, and helped the man to get work. His wife and children were sent for. He was encouraged to go on relating his experience. He became a minister, and wrote one hymn, " Out of darkness into light." Name : O. W. Littimore.

The hymn that helped to save him was written by a woman, always an invalid, never having known, as she once said, an hour of health in all her life.

> God moves in a mysterious way,
>   His wonders to perform ;
> He plants His footsteps in the sea,
>   And rides upon the storm.

Another case.—A Lawyer, in America, who sank so low as to become a tramp in the streets of New York. He was 55 years old, and homeless and penniless. He was passing the Florence Mission. The window was open and they were singing :

> Once again the gospel message
>   From the Saviour you have heard ;
> Will you heed the invitation,
>   Will you turn, and seek the Lord ?

It came like the voice of God to him. His early training had been Christian, and he thought he would go in. He did so, and as he took his seat the audience was singing the second verse :—

> Many summers you have wasted,
>   Ripened Harvest you have seen ;
> Winter snows, by spring have melted,
>   Yet you linger in your sin.

He realised that this was a truthful picture of his own life, and listened to the third verse, ending :—

> While the Spirit now is striving,
>   Yield, and seek the Saviour's side.

Deeply convicted, he jumped to his feet, and said : " I will yield ; I will seek the Saviour's side."

He was converted. He secured good employment, became reconciled to his wife and family, returned to his old home, where he lived an earnest Christian.

Jesus can save the worst of men if they will only let Him.

LOVE, AND WHAT IT CAN DO.

Norman Macleod, while in his Highland Parish, tells of a widow unable to pay her rent, and threatened with eviction. She sets out one day with her only child to walk ten miles over the mountain to the home of friends who were able to help her.

When she started the weather was warm and bright, but on the mountain she was caught in a terrible snowstorm.

A Prayer That Saved.

Mr. Lionel B. Fletcher, who is conducting the *New Life* Campaign under the auspices of a Congregational Committee, has for seven years been the Pastor of Wood Street Congregational Church, Cardiff

He is proving to be a very successful Evangelist.

As a boy, he thought he would like to be a sailor. Arrangements were made for him to go to sea. Father and mother were some time before they could say yes. But when they got to know that the Captain was a Christian, they consented.

He refers to the last breakfast he had at home. After breakfast, reading and prayer.

When we knelt for the prayer, he says, there followed a silence, like death. For quite a while my father could not command his voice, and that silence will remain with me till I can remember nothing. Then I heard his voice, thick with emotion, as he just said : " Loving God." There was another terrible silence. The sobs began to jump from my throat. Then I heard my father's chair move, and I knew he was coming towards me. The next moment his arm was about my neck, and I felt his wet cheek against mine. Immediately he began to pray again. " Loving God, preserve this boy from the sins which will face him. Keep him pure. Grant that he may come back to us untarnished, for Christ's sake, Amen."

That prayer moulded my future more than any prayer he had ever uttered. I took with me a written document which I had signed, with my father and mother as witnesses, in which I promised certain things concerning my conduct.

But a lad of 16 rarely remains in the same mood for long. The new life interested me and kept me busy. I began to mix with the men. I was naturally full of life and vigour. My temper was quick and sometimes my tongue was quicker still.

Then came a night on which I was to join in some plan which had been laid. I rushed into my cabin for my cap, and as I drew back the curtains of my bunk, the light of the lamp fell full on the photograph of my father. It was tacked up on the wall of the bunk, and the eyes seemed alive, and the face quivering. I felt his arm about me, and heard again the voice. " Loving God, preserve this, my boy, from the sins which will face him. Keep him pure. Grant that he may come back to us untarnished. For Christ's sake, Amen." I fell on my knees, and, with a sob, I said, " I won't do it, dad." And I have kept my promise.

Ps. 103, and the 4th verse, have always been precious to me since then.

Who redeemeth thy life from destruction.

In an hour when some temptation besets us, it is of great assistance to us to think, it may be, of some one who loves us, of some one who is going to be hurt were we to fail, of some shadow which will pass over another's face; it may be the face of a friend, or it may be the face of God.

Jesus, if we will permit Him, will, by the very look upon His face, guide us, and lead us into the path of safety.

THE ORGANIST AND THE MASTER MUSICIAN.

There is a story told of a village organist, who one day was practising on the Church organ. He was playing a piece of that master of music, Mendelssohn, and was not playing it very well.

A stranger sat in the back pew of the Church. He heard the imperfections of the player, and when he stopped playing he made bold to step forward and asked : " Sir, would you allow me to play ? " The man said, gruffly, " Certainly not. I never allow anyone to touch the organ but myself." " I should be glad if you would allow me the privilege." Again the man gave a gruff refusal. After the third request the appeal was granted, but most ungraciously. The stranger sat down, pulled out the stops, and began to play the same piece on the same instrument. But what a change. It was as though the Church was filled with heavenly music. The organist said, " Who are you ?" The modest stranger replied, " My name is Mendelssohn." " What, did I refuse you permission to play on my organ ? "

That is what many do with Jesus Christ. He wants to take the instrument of our life and bring out all the beautiful harmony there is stored into it, but which we cannot of ourselves produce. Will you let Him do it ? It is for this He calls you to come to Him, that He may make your life useful and happy.

THE WORKING OF GOD IN THE HUMAN HEART.

I have made use of the following story to show the working of God in the human heart.

Two Americans were once crossing the Atlantic, and met in the cabin on Sunday night to sing hymns. As they sang the last hymn, " Jesus, Lover of my soul," one of them heard an exceeding rich and beautiful voice behind him. He looked around, and, although he did not know the face, he thought that he knew the voice. So, when the music ceased, he turned and asked the man if he had been in the Civil War.

The man replied that he had been a Confederate soldier.

" Were you at such a place at such a night ? " asked the first.

" Yes," he replied, " and a curious thing happened that night which this hymn has recalled to my mind. I was posted on sentry duty near the edge of a wood. It was a dark night and very cold, and I was a little frightened because the enemy were supposed to be very near. About midnight, when everything was very still and I was feeling homesick, and miserable and weary, I thought that I would comfort myself by praying and singing a hymn. I remember singing this hymn :

> ' All my trust on Thee is stayed,
>   All my help from Thee I bring ;
> Cover my defenceless head
>   With the shadow of Thy wing.'

After singing that, a strange peace came down upon me, and through the long night I felt no more fear."

" Now," said the other, " listen to my story. I was a Union soldier, and was in the wood that night with a party of scouts. I saw you standing, although I did not see your face. My men had their rifles focused upon you, waiting the word to fire, but when you sang out :

> ' Cover my defenceless head
>   With the shadow of Thy wing '

I said : ' Boys, lower your rifles ; we will go home."
It was God working in each of them.   All through a hymn.

In my early ministry I read several of Dr. Richard Newton's Books, an American clergyman, and I have given in my sermons and addresses many interesting and helpful stories by him.

" The Steamboat Captain and the Soldier," and " The Result of Early Choice," are Dr. Newton's.

The Steamboat Captain and the Soldier.

During the late war there was a steamboat one day in front of a flourishing town on the Ohio river.   The captain who had charge of her was the owner of the boat.   The steam was up ; and the captain was about to start on a trip some miles down the river, with an excursion party, who had chartered the boat for the occasion.   While waiting for the party to come on board, a poor soldier came up to the captain.   He said he was suffering from severe sickness, as well as from his wounds.   He had been in the hospital.   The doctor had told him that he could not live long ; and he was very anxious to get home, and see his mother again before he died ; and he wished to know if the captain would give him a passage down the river on his boat.   On hearing where his home was, the captain said that the party who had chartered his boat were going near that place; and he told the poor soldier that he would gladly take him to his home.

But when the excursion party came on board, and saw the soldier, with his soiled and worn clothes, and his ugly-looking wounds, they were not willing to let him go, and asked the captain to put him ashore. The captain told the soldier's sad story, and pleaded his cause very earnestly. He said he would place him on the lower deck, and put a screen round his bed, so that they could not see him. But the young people refused. They said, as they had hired the boat, it belonged to them for the day, and they were not willing to have such a miserable-looking object on board their boat; and that if the captain did not put him off, they would hire another boat, and he would lose the twenty dollars they had agreed to give him for the day's excursion.

The good captain made one more appeal to them He asked them to put themselves in the poor soldier's place, and then to think how they would like to be treated. But still they refused to let the soldier go. Then the noble-hearted captain said :" Well, ladies and gentlemen, whether you hire my boat or not, I intend to take this soldier home to-day."

The party did hire another boat. The captain lost his twenty dollars. But when he returned the poor dying soldier to the arms of his loving mother, he felt that the tears of gratitude with which she thanked him were worth more than the money he had lost. The gentle mother dressed the wounds of her poor suffering boy; and nursed and cared for him, as none but a mother knows how to do.

rooms.   The other man said he was in debt and could not leave.   No. 1 went out of the room and paid the man's bill, sent for a carriage, bundled up his bits of things, and took him to his lodgings.

No. 2 made several slips, but No. 1 never let him go. No. 1 passed a fairly good examination   No. 2, the man who was almost lost, graduated with honours.

The last time I heard of No. 1, says Drummond, he was filling an important appointment in London.

No. 2 is known as the Christian Doctor of a Village in Wales.

It must have been a great joy to No. 1 having been the means of saving No. 2, body and soul.

God uses the events of life in winning souls to Himself, and helping believers.

It was God who prompted No. 1 to do what he did for No. 2.

It is good business to devote our lives to individuals.   By giving we get.   No. 1 was a better man after saving No. 2.

A WORD TO BELIEVERS AND CHRISTIAN WORKERS.

I have tried in the sermonettes to simplify the plan of salvation, showing what Christ is willing to do for us, the help He is ready to give, viz : The gift of Himself. And there must be a willingness on our part to give ourselves to Him and His service. He wants us to become co-workers.

A true Christian life is one that has come under new influences, that is in reality a new life, a divine principle, entering the heart and changing all within and then without. It is heaven, not merely lying about a man, but entering into him and permeating his whole life.

Religion, therefore, takes hold upon the life and leaves its seal upon the character.

To you who have taken the Lord Jesus Christ for your Redeemer, He is also your High Priest. His great business in heaven to-day is to represent you, your needs, your infirmities, and your trials. I want you to know this very fully, for no other truth can give you more daily comfort, or more firmly establish you in a constant holy walk. Having died to save you, Jesus lives to keep you.

I exhort the young men to be sober. Exercise yourselves unto Godliness ; run the race according to Paul's

motto, looking unto Jesus. Draw your inspiration and
power directly from Himself.

I would to God that I might help you to see the glory of
Christian service.

There are some, perhaps, who are a little weary and tired.
You teach in the Sunday School, and you wonder whether
the toil and drudgery are worth while. Lift your service
and look at it in the light of these great words : " My Father
worketh even until now, and I work."

" Working together with Him ! " Therein is the glory
of service.

" Working together with Him ! " That is the story of
what you are doing. Dear tired heart, it is not just a class
in the Sunday School ; do not speak of your work that way.
If some one should ask you what part you take in church
work, do not say you only take a class; say that you work
with God. If you can so work through all the years as to
get one child-heart and teach it to trust, you will have done
work that angels might envy.

> " O the joy of saving souls,
>   Think of it."

There is nothing to be compared with this. One soul
lifted by the power of your instrumentality and the blessing
of God into a sphere of immortality and glory, shall shine
as the stars in the firmament ; such achievements will be
a source of more joy when you stand in Zion and before
God, than all the treasures of the world. " They that be
wise shall shine as the brightness of the firmament ; and
they that turn many to righteousness, as the stars for ever
and ever."

You are not only working for time, but for eternity; polishing stones for the heavenly temple, and searching for gems with which to deck the Saviour's crown.

Do not measure the beginnings of Divine life in yourself by the end of Divine life in other people. You are called, not to a consummation; you are called, not to a spiritual banquet, to which you are to sit down, dismissing all care; you are called to education. You are to begin with the alphabet, you are to learn to spell the smallest spiritual words and you are to go from step to step, and from strength to strength, till you come to a perfect manhood in Christ Jesus.

" If I can put one touch of a rosy sunset into the life of any man or woman, I shall feel that I have worked with God."

A FINAL WORD.

The beauty of Christ attracted me in early life, and I am still in love with Him after sixty years.

If God spares me, I shall shortly pass the 79th mile stone of my life, and I stand to-day on the mountain top, a kind of borderland between two worlds.

What I have seen enables me to trust God for what I have not seen. I appeal to preachers, especially young preachers, at all cost to get to know Jesus Christ. Drink in the Pauline spirit of complete surrender to Christ. Think His thoughts, breathe His atmosphere, be content to proclaim His Evangel. Thus will you reach life's highest ideal. Then with joyous and confident emphasis you will be able to say: I have not run in vain, neither laboured in vain.

My ministerial life has been one ray of sunshine. Whatever of life still remains to me I give it to Him without stint.

Living or dying, I am the Lord's. Thou, O Christ, art all I want.